THE POWER OF COACHING

THE POWER OF COACHING

NURTURING LEADERSHIP & PERSONAL DEVELOPMENT

OPTIMUS COACH ACADEMY
ALUMNI AUTHORS

authors
AND CO.

First published in Great Britain in 2024
by Authors & Co.
www.authorsandco.pub

ISBN 978-1-915771-64-3 (paperback)

Disclaimer

In parts throughout this book, the authors may have tried to recreate events, locales and conversations from their memories of them. In order to maintain their anonymity, in some instances we have changed the names of individuals and places, and we may have changed some identifying characteristics and details such as physical properties, occupations and places of residence. Although the co-authors and publisher have made every effort to ensure that the information in this book was correct at press time, the co-authors and publisher do not assume and hereby disclaim any liability to any party for any loss, damage, or disruption caused by errors or omissions, whether such errors or omissions result from negligence, accident, or any other cause.

CONTENTS

1

INTRODUCTION — RUTH KUDZI

Coaching can help change the way people think, feel and act. It supports people to make new connections in their brains so they re-wire them from the inside out.

I have worked with thousands of clients and seen huge transformations. In leading the writing of this book, I wanted to bring to life the impact coaching can have from a range of perspectives.

This book brings together ten skilful coaches who delve into how coaching has helped them and others to show you how the skill of coaching can be adapted to meet differing needs and audiences. Coaching can be transformational both for the people who are being coached and for those who are doing the work and becoming coaches.

The term *coaching* is not protected and although we stick to the ICF definition of coaching in our work at Optimus Coach Academy, there is fluidity even in this. In practice, we often integrate coaching in a personalised manner, dependent on the needs of the individual and organisation.

Coaching is client-centred, non-directional and forward-focused: skilful coaches see the whole person and adapt their approach to meet the needs of that person in front of them. The impact on people of great coaching means it is now the second-fastest growing industry in the world.

I am passionate about the industry, given my own personal experience alongside decades of training. I grew up thinking I was different which made me choose to study Psychology from the age of sixteen. Looking back, I realise I didn't fit in because there were a lot of things going on in my life, alongside neuro-divergence. I struggled with my mental health from a young age: I had anxiety and spells of depression. After a tragic accident when I was eighteen I suffered from complex PTSD and often drank, partied or shopped in my attempt to feel better, which didn't really work. I was curious about personal development and understanding people as I wanted to understand myself and feel less like a misfit.

I first heard about coaching back in the 1990s while studying Psychology and Management at the University of Leeds. Our lecturer described the most effective leadership styles and talked about a coaching approach which differed from the more traditional directive models. I already had experience of working with a directive boss (and rebelling against it) so my ears pricked up: to me this made so much sense.

Over the years I imagined becoming a life coach and immersed myself in reading about personal development, studying more Psychology and doing mindfulness training. It was at a festival a few years after finishing my degree that I met two people who were coaches and it started to seem like a career in coaching was possible. Back then, I felt I needed to get my life more in order before I was able to help others, despite the fact I was a teacher! Now I know coaching isn't about teaching people based on my experience, it is about how I support others to find their answers. Our personal experiences can be important in helping us connect and have empathy with others, yet we don't need to be the finished article – if that even exists. It is all about being a work in progress.

A few years later, studying for a Master's Degree in Psychology and Education, I became interested in growth mindset and Neuroplasticity. I found myself in a lecture as part of a leadership development programme. Coaching was not only the core methodology by which we developed leadership skills but also as one of the most effective ways we could manage and lead teams within education.

I had my first coach and started training in coaching skills. I soon began using these in my role (and getting much better results with my team) and I was building my confidence as a coach. I soon began to offer leadership coaching within my network and started to do additional training: I'd found my thing. As an educator I'd always loved seeing people get their own results and learn new things, and coaching seemed like a natural progression.

By working with a coach I was finally able to move forward from PTSD and changed my life around. I no longer drank to excess and I curbed my spending. I now live with my family in my dream house in a beautiful area and have a great network. I always had the network but many other things hadn't been working. Coaching changed how I felt about myself, made me recognise the potential I had, and helped me be more positive. I knew if it had helped me it could help others too.

A few years later I enrolled in an ICF coach training course and later a post-grad in coaching and soon left my senior leadership role to start my own coaching business. I then recognised the need for great coach training and wanted to provide something based on Psychology and Neuroscience which would help people become great coaches and have a massive impact. I started this in 2019 and we've now trained over one thousand coaches worldwide as well as thousands more in organisations through our programmes.

I love the discipline of coaching as it is flexible and focused on the individual – and it has changed my life: everyone can benefit from coaching as what you are really doing is unlocking all the things you have inside you.

I have found over the last three decades of exploring Psychology and Human Behaviour and training to be an ICF-accredited master coach that the biggest development is self-development: the ability to be comfortable in yourself and to have conversations without ego where you're not the centre of attention makes a huge difference.

Interestingly a meta-analysis of studies published in 2023 found that coaching had a positive impact across studies irrespective of what was being measured. At some level what we measure or focus on develops and this is consistent across self, peer and manager feedback: we know coaching works as an intervention. The chapters that follow offer you vignettes, case studies and examples of effective coaching.

One of the themes of this book is that coaching works across contexts and is useful for marginalised groups. Whether we look through a DEI lens or focus on neurodivergent people, coaching helps people to be more authentically them. If coaching was integrated into school curriculums, many people could feel more confident and resilient which would have a positive impact on outcomes and the community. Most people disengage when they feel excluded or don't feel things are for them. Whilst it is true that there are real structural barriers to many people achieving, coaching could help empower everyone.

This book explores coaching with adults through the lens of ten coaches and how they use this skill to support others. You will see a passion for working with people to help them to unlock their potential. You'll see how each coach has their own approach with their clients which includes empathy, compassion and challenge.

If you are considering receiving coaching or training as a coach, these perspectives will help you recognise that the power of coaching comes from the power of individual autonomy and choice and of being listened to and seen for who you are. When I train coaches I tell them one of the reasons coaching is so impactful is that you are being listened to without judgement – which is unfortunately harder and harder to find in our society.

Space to air your thoughts and feelings and to recognise what is going on in your body can in itself be transformative. With awareness comes clarity and then you can focus on what you want to change. We often get stuck in patterns we are unaware. We are often in a state of *react rather than respond*: space to explore what is going on and to recognise why we do things can help transform our behaviour.

Some coaches who have contributed to this book are relatively new to the discipline, while others have decades of experience.

You'll notice that although all have gone through high level training with Optimus, each brings their own style and experience to what they do and they have chosen to work in different ways. I also love coaching for its flexibility. It is not prescriptive and you can combine it with other appropriate modalities.

ABOUT RUTH KUDZI

CEO + Course Director, MCC Coach

Ruth is a well respected and successful coach who has worked across sectors including leadership, career and more recently business and mindset. She has over 10,000 coaching hours and has completed hundreds of hours of training and coaching supervision. Ruth is a MCC level coach with the ICF and is our course director and CEO. Prior to becoming a coach Ruth was a senior leader in education.

Website: https://www.optimuscoachacademy.com

instagram.com/ruthkudzi
linkedin.com/in/ruthkudzi

2

THE POWER OF PERSONAL AND PROFESSIONAL GROWTH THROUGH COACHING — ADAM CENEY

CLEARING UP A MIDDLE AGED MAN'S MISUNDERSTANDING

Coaching isn't just a tool; it's a superpower. It is the kind of power that can reshape careers, elevate individuals, and revolutionise teams. I firmly believe that access to coaching should be universal, for individuals navigating their personal journeys, and for organisations seeking to unleash their team's full potential.

Yet, I am compelled to question: How many people do you know who have received a profound impact through a coach? Have you experienced the benefits yourself? How many organisations can you think of which have actively harnessed the potential of coaching for specific challenges, either through in-house experts or external partners?

Until a few years ago, I hadn't received coaching, at least not consciously. I wonder if the cause of its perceived limited reach is two-fold. First, coaching often gets entangled with other modalities such as counselling and mentoring, creating a cloud of confusion. Second, in a world driven by immediate results, the magic that coaching can weave might not always be apparent. It is a challenge to believe in and engage with a process that creates things from previous invisibility.

Coaching stands distinct from counselling and mentoring. It doesn't merely illuminate; it empowers individuals to recognise and seize their potential. It does not just provide us with additional awareness; it allows us to leverage that awareness to navigate a new course of action.

Unlike traditional learning exercises confined to a classroom, coaching is a dynamic journey that extends beyond the coaching session. It instils strategies and confidence, propelling individuals toward futures they felt were impossible – too ambitious for them to achieve.

I've homed in on supporting individuals at the mid-point of their careers who feel lost and adrift of who they are. I guide them through a process that brings clarity to their thoughts, unveils their unique value and empowers them to design careers that align with their lives on their terms.

This commitment stems from my own personal experience—coaching altered my trajectory, and as such I'm a firm believer that, regardless of your current situation, you can craft and move closer to the future of your choosing.

The people I work with often present specific goals—rediscovering their identity, pursuing a promotion, or embarking on a new career direction. While common themes emerge, coaching refuses a one-size-fits-all approach. There are frameworks to guide the process, but the coach's role is to listen, enquire and empower a person to own their solutions, progress and outcomes.

I get the most joy out of being a coach when I witness the moments someone's eyes light up with newfound realisations, and I observe the evolution of their approach and behaviour, having experienced it from the other side, or when I receive messages between sessions which celebrate their self-designed victories. I have come to see coaching not just as a process but as a catalyst for profound personal and professional growth.

But it wasn't always this way. My perspectives on coaching have evolved significantly, shaped by overcoming misconceptions that once hindered my engagement. In this chapter, I'll delve into these misunderstandings and illustrate what can be achieved not only through being coached but also by embracing a coaching mindset. Prepare to discover the untapped power within and the superpower that is coaching.

It would be wrong to say I always saw coaching as a superpower.

If you had asked me a few years ago what I thought of coaching, I'd have given you a different answer. Not because the world of coaching has suddenly changed but because I didn't comprehend it or the impact it can have.

If I'm honest, I might have pooh-poohed it. I probably did pooh-pooh it because that's what you do with things you don't understand, right? Like all things we don't understand, the associations we create with them never change until they are challenged, and my previous associations with coaching were very different.

My association with coaching was firmly rooted in the world of sports. Picture it: eager dads, clad head-to-toe in tracksuits (the fashion of the early nineties), braving all kinds of weather on muddy, uneven fields, attempting to nurture the next football prodigies. Their advice often boiled down to classics like, "When in doubt, kick it out." Amidst the mud and chaos, the most critical decision of the day was, "Do we play uphill or downhill in the first half?"

For me, coaching meant instruction and guidance, plain and simple. But as I grew older, I encountered a broader definition of coaching, one that extended beyond the sports arena. And yet, even though I considered myself open to new ideas, I pigeonholed coaching outside of sports into one specific category: life coaching.

Now, I'll probably regret what I'm about to say, but it is the truth. When I heard the term "life coaching," my imagination conjured up images of people frolicking barefoot in flowery meadows and talk of energy streams. It is a real aspect of some coaching and I'm not mocking it if that is your thing. My point is that coaching is a much bigger landscape than I had explored.

There's no sugar-coating how I got there—it wasn't a fairy tale journey, one to be shared at bedtime. I went through a mentally challenging time. It was as if I'd been meandering through life, and then, in my mid-thirties, I reached a point of reckoning. By conventional standards, my career might have looked successful. In many ways, it had been.

I had diligently followed the well-trodden path of career progression, seizing every new role and opportunity that came my way. However, at the midpoint of my career, I felt not the thrill of accomplishment, but a sense of entrapment and disillusionment. I ticked all the boxes of societal norms, but realised I'd been doing it all wrong—at least wrong for me.

I found myself in a state of stagnation, utterly lost, and emotionally burnt out. I felt overwhelmingly that I had no real options for changing my situation. It took me a while, a bit too long perhaps, to admit I had a problem. Eventually, I took a step forward and sought solace in counselling.

Counselling was a valuable starting point which allowed me to make sense of my situation and offered strategies to cope. It served its purpose at the time, but it was limited by its focus on what had happened in the past that affected the now. Then, when the world was struck by a pandemic and we all found ourselves in lockdown, I embraced a newfound sense of curiosity and committed to personal development.

My daily routine began with an hour dedicated to learning something new, an experience that proved to be liberating. During this period of exploration, the "aha" moment materialised, quite by accident, unless you're a believer in fate or serendipity.

One day, a video by a coach named Michael Neill caught my eye. He delved into the concept of living life from the "inside out" rather than the "outside in.". It struck a chord with me. I've since come to explain it as the difference between my experience of a roller coaster and my son's experience of it. The physical ride is the same, but our perceptions are entirely distinct. He is thrilled, while I am terrified. This revelation made me realise that our experiences are often created in our minds, not solely dictated by external circumstances.

It might have been a clever algorithm or simply my brain making a valuable connection. Regardless, I delved deeper into this concept, found that it shed light on what I hadn't quite grasped through counselling, and something clicked for me.

This revelation led me to the next step: seeking a coach for myself.

I ventured into the realm of coaching with a mix of excitement and anxiety. The first proper online coaching session was an intriguing blend of emotions. The coach and I had already engaged in a discovery call, but an actual session had its distinct aura, although I took an odd sense of comfort from the fact that I remained in the familiar confines of my own home.

During my recent exploration of personal development, I had encountered coaches (like Michael Neill) but because of the way I was consuming their content, it was still focused on imparting knowledge and guiding me to develop specific skills. In that context, my role as a coachee was clear—I was there to absorb and be shaped by the wisdom and concepts being offered by the experienced coach. But being coached brought me a different experience.

While I had an understanding of what coaching should be, I wasn't fully prepared for the experience that awaited me. Fortunately, the coach I had was extraordinary, and it didn't take me long to realise how strikingly different this would be from my expectations. Instead of dwelling on past events, venting about my challenges, or being told the answers, coaching focused solely on me and my vision of the future. This forward-oriented approach is often overlooked in our day-to-day lives.

It's strange to think about it now, especially after becoming a certified and accredited coach, but that simple yet powerful question, "What would you like to focus on today?" was quite new to me back then. In every session, I set the focus, articulated why it was important to me, and described what I wanted to change. The freedom to explore, free of judgement and the coach's steerage toward solutions, was truly liberating.

At times, it felt like an almost mystical art—an experience that's challenging to convey to others if they haven't immersed themselves in it. The "me" of years gone by might have responded to a coach with scepticism, and asked, "So, you just listen to people, ask a few questions, and they find answers and solutions from within to move forward?"

Within these coaching sessions, there were moments when things just clicked and solutions that had once seemed impossible were now crystal clear, almost by magic. As I began witnessing the positive transformations not only in my personal life but also in my professional endeavours, a new determination took hold. I wanted to learn how to wield this powerful tool for the benefit of others, and that's when I started to look at becoming a coach.

The story could end there, right? I had struggles and misunderstandings, but I did some learning, and finally found what I wanted to do so it was all fine...except things don't usually conclude neatly like that. How many times do we find ourselves knowing exactly what we want, only to be thwarted by invisible barriers that keep us from taking action?

Whilst we don't want to face any barriers once we decide what we want, they do exist. Addressing them effectively is crucial if you want to follow through with your desires for change. I wasn't immune so here are some of the barriers a middle-aged man (me) had to address to be able to move towards the future in coaching he wanted.

I still felt a stigma around my mental health and the challenges I'd faced. Whilst stigma affects both men and women, there were, and still is to some extent, traditional gender roles and societal expectations that often discourage men from seeking help or support. Even as I engaged with a coach and made my own moves into coaching, I still held a fear of being weak and vulnerable around other people. I wanted others to perceive me as self-reliant… stoic, even.

I also had to find the right training path. There were so many different options and approaches that it felt overwhelming. Type 'coach training' into a search engine and you'll be presented with millions of hits and an array of training providers offering a multitude of approaches. I became certain I wanted something that meant I was not only certified but would have the ability to become accredited with a professional body. Even this wasn't without its considerations: there is the International Coaching Federation (ICF), the European Mentoring and Coaching Council (EMCC) and the Association of Coaching (AC).

I spoke to my coach about their experiences, their journey, what they did, and how they found things (I know that is technically mentoring!) and we had sessions that helped me focus on what was right for me.

I knew what I wanted, I knew why I wanted it, and I knew where I was able to get it.

I had just one final thing to sort out to make it a reality. I needed to find the time to do the training, which meant I needed to reconsider how I was working. I didn't want to train in the evenings after a day's work as I would be unable to focus properly. Weekends were too packed with family activities to commit to months of weekly training.

I wanted to dedicate a day each week to coaching and my only option was to reduce the number of days I worked. There would be an inevitable financial impact but what held me back most was how it would be perceived in my professional life. In hindsight, this was another of my own hang-ups. I found my employers were far more accepting and accommodating than I'd given them credit for in my head.

These obstacles, both internal and external, were part and parcel of my journey. Overcoming them demanded resilience, understanding, and determination. They underscore the truth that personal and professional growth often come with a set of unique challenges to be met head-on.

By venturing into the world of coaching, a transformation had already begun. I had successfully navigated a challenging period in my life, and now, I felt a renewed spring in my step. The journey from uncertainty to rediscovering my passion was well underway, and the upcoming nine months of training were my next destination.

A tangible marker of this shift was the creation of a limited company for my coaching practice. This encapsulated my commitment to this newfound path. I had already enrolled in the course, but I didn't want to lose momentum. So, I embarked on the journey of establishing a coaching business, from selecting the name to official registration at Companies House.

You might wonder why I took this step so early. It was my way of wholeheartedly committing to the ideas that had been taking shape in my mind about becoming a coach. Surprisingly, the process was remarkably straightforward and reinforced my belief in the direction I was heading. It was an affirmation of my dedication to this transformative journey, a tangible symbol of my determination to embrace coaching as a way of life.

Yet as I began the coaching course, a familiar sense of anxiety washed over me. Doubts crept in, and the inner sceptic started to stir. However, I was reassured by the sense of belonging I found within the incredible group I was in.

We were on a shared journey, each with our unique circumstances, yet bound together by common themes. I had underestimated the value of this community at the beginning. It wasn't just a class; it was a network of like-minded individuals who were there to support, practise, and put the theory we were learning into action. It was a reminder of the importance of community, of the bonds we form, and the profound impact of human connection, even in the virtual realm.

We can certainly learn things on our own, but I've come to realise that progress is much slower when we choose the solitary path. In fact, I might not have achieved what I have in the last few years.

I wonder if you ever experience the same sense of urgency I sometimes grapple with. I get the feeling that things should be moving faster than they are. I often create the illusion that I'm lagging behind, that I should be further along, and that I should possess more knowledge than I do. This is where the incredible community that surrounded me proved invaluable. It didn't erase those feelings, but it equipped me to recognise them, to build awareness of their origin, and to challenge them.

Understanding my own behaviour has aided my personal growth and enabled me to identify these patterns in the people I work with. We frequently possess the insight to guide others but struggle to find solutions for our own challenges. One of the most profound benefits of being both a coach and a learner of coaching is the development of self-awareness. You discover who you are, what you value, and why your chosen focus matters deeply to you. This self-awareness serves as an anchor when the world doesn't align with your expectations, and offers clarity and guidance in times of uncertainty.

I learned a lot about myself during training, both as a coach and as someone being coached. Through these experiences, I learned what worked and what didn't, not just for me but for the people I was coaching.

The training introduced me to a wide array of coaching approaches, ranging from fundamental yet highly effective models like GROW to the realms of positive psychology, neuroscience, and transactional analysis techniques. My coach trainer aptly described it as having a wardrobe of concepts that you can reach for and apply when the situation demands it.

This learning process was neither immediate nor linear, despite my inherent sense of urgency. Time played a crucial role in internalising and applying newfound knowledge, in stark contrast to the fleeting nature of day courses, where you acquire knowledge but lack the opportunity to test, refine, and question it. I've had too many experiences like this that led to the possession of a certificate without a practical application of what I learned.

As for that relentless inner voice that whispers doubts about readiness and worthiness, I've come to understand that when you embark on something new, you're likely to be far from perfect at the outset. And that's perfectly okay. The most challenging part is taking the first step. Once you do, you find yourself entering what Brendan Burchard calls the "confidence-competence loop".

Reflect on any skill or knowledge you've acquired; think back to the moment you began. The more you engage in something, the more proficient you become, and this, in turn, boosts your confidence. This heightened confidence encourages you to explore new opportunities, creating a positive feedback loop that propels your growth and learning journey.

From the coach training onwards, a ripple effect started to occur not just within me, but in the environments and situations I found myself. I now see the impact on the people I coach.

For me, the power of coaching transcended far beyond the personal; it broke me free from the societal stereotypes, real and perceived, that restrained me. Growing up and living exclusively in Western culture, I often felt the weight of society's expectations, dictating how I should behave, express emotions, and make life choices. These constraints had limited my ability to explore my full potential.

Coaching offered me a safe and non-judgemental space to challenge these stereotypes so I could redefine my identity and embrace my authentic self. This self-reflection and introspection helped me develop a deeper understanding of my values, desires, and aspirations, and led me to a more fulfilling and purpose-driven life.

I was able to develop my emotional intelligence and effective communication skills. Instead of being discouraged from openly expressing my emotions or seeking support, the coaching environment encouraged me to explore my emotions, develop self-awareness, and cultivate healthier ways of expressing myself. Whilst this will always be a work in progress, I was no longer suppressing my emotions and putting up communication barriers, which had caused me problems in the past. I was enhancing my relationships, building stronger connections, and navigating conflicts more effectively.

Being coached enabled me to navigate my career. I gained clarity on my professional goals, identified my strengths and weaknesses, and developed strategies to overcome obstacles. Throughout, I knew someone had my back to provide guidance, accountability, and support.

I knew I had a delicate balance between work and personal life to manage. Whilst I wanted a professional life, I also wanted a family life. I had to redefine my relationship with what I did and when I did it, set boundaries, and prioritise myself; this meant I could achieve a healthier work-life integration than I'd ever had before.

No matter who you are, life can be full of challenges and setbacks. No one is immune to them, including me. Thanks to coaching, I now possess the tools and mindset to build resilience and confront difficult situations with confidence. I've cultivated problem-solving skills, learned to manage stress effectively, and shattered self-limiting beliefs that once held me back.

Coaching has been the catalyst that unlocked my potential, fostered my personal growth, and imbued me with the resolve and resilience to confront challenges head-on. It is a transformative force that has shaped my own world and I now use IT to impact the lives of those I now coach.

I couldn't have accomplished any of this alone, no matter how many resources were at my disposal. That's one of the remarkable aspects of the coaching community—it's a group of individuals always ready to lend a helping hand. I was genuinely surprised and pleased by the absence of cutthroat competition in the coaching community I became a part of. It is perfectly acceptable to serve the same people and to offer coaching in the same industry. It is alright to acknowledge when you might not be the perfect fit for a client but know someone who is. It is fine to collaborate and to support one another. I had never encountered a world like this before, having spent years in competitive, politically charged environments where one misstep could easily lead to sidelining.

And coaches, like everyone else, need coaching themselves, whether through direct coaching or supervision. We practise what we preach because, even though we possess the skills and techniques to work through issues, we are as human as anyone else. Even as I ventured into coaching, I grappled with some limiting beliefs. I knew who my ideal coaching clients should be, but I doubted my ability to convey this effectively to people.

With the support of my fellow coaches, I worked through these challenges. In fact, the mere fact I am writing this—something I would do but never share in the past—demonstrates my breakthrough in overcoming long-held barriers.

It was now time to find out who I wanted to coach. I began by practising with fellow coaches experiencing a similar learning curve. We provided each other support, driven by our shared eagerness to learn and apply our newfound knowledge in real-world scenarios. It took me some time to pinpoint the specific focus I wanted for my coaching, but I eventually realised I wanted to help people avoid finding themselves in the position I had been in a few years back. Burnout is a serious issue, and its warning signs often manifest well before the critical point.

With growing confidence and a clearer sense of direction in my coaching, I took on pro-bono clients. This allowed me to practise coaching on non-coaches, a valuable step towards accreditation with the ICF. You can have up to thirty hours recorded for the Associate Certified Coach level, and it made perfect sense to start here. Through these sessions, I began to find my rhythm and discover tools and techniques that were effective for those people.

I started noticing common themes among the people who sought my coaching services. I recognised in them some of the struggles I had faced in the past, and this led me to become more focused on helping individuals at the midpoint of their careers who feel lost in their professional paths. My mission became clear: I help them gain clarity in their thinking, uncover their unique value, and create a career that aligns with the life they currently have or aspire to achieve on their own terms.

My coaching practice has evolved alongside my day-to-day work. Without the training and coaching I received, I wouldn't have made the significant progress I've experienced over the past few years. I remain open, curious, and committed to continual learning and growth as a coach. Achieving a certificate and accreditation is not the end, it's just the beginning of my vision to make coaching widely understood for what it truly is and what it can accomplish.

I want people, particularly men edging towards the position I found myself in a few years back, to be aware of the benefits of engaging with coaching much earlier so they don't have the same uphill battles. Maybe like me, they misunderstand the concept of coaching as something exclusively for athletes or executives in professional roles. It isn't. Everyone can access the benefits of coaching at any stage of life.

I want coaching to be accessible and available to the widest possible group of people. Its utility can be applied to individuals and teams and could be the secret to unlocking so much potential. We are no longer bound by the limitations of physical space or time zones. I have coached people from all over the world and it is still effective.

I believe in the importance of emotional well-being and self-improvement, and I want to help shift societal norms, encourage everyone to seek coaching without fear of judgement, and ultimately create an inclusive and supportive environment where everyone can feel comfortable seeking coaching.

On an individual level, I want to see more people wake up every morning with a spring in their step, knowing that their day at work is going to be amazing. I want people to feel in control of their careers, having crafted their work activities and relationships to provide them with a sense of purpose and belonging.

I want to see more people smiling gleefully as they recount their experiences and personal development, all made possible because their careers offer a profound sense of accomplishment and satisfaction.

Everyone can have the opportunity to grow, learn, and expand their expertise, advancing in environments where they are valued and recognised for who they are and what they can achieve. This can be accomplished without compromising a healthy work-life balance that allows individuals to manage their time, set boundaries, and maintain a sustainable equilibrium that fits their unique situation.

I have achieved this, and it is my mission to use coaching as a means to help others attain it as well.

I stand here today, a testament to the transformative powers of coaching and the extraordinary revelations it has unfurled not only within me but in those that I now coach and serve. It has the potential to be a transformative experience for everyone, including middle-aged men like me, to be empowered to break free from societal stereotypes, enhance emotional intelligence, navigate career transitions, achieve work-life integration, and build resilience.

The path to becoming a coach, much like life itself, was marked with doubts, hesitations, and questions seeking elusive answers. Yet, every step of this unearthed the immense potential that resides within me and every one of us. Coaching is not just a profession; it is a calling and a mission to help others navigate their own unique paths.

Coaching is an art of asking questions, sparking insights, and enabling individuals to access their inner wisdom. It is a journey from uncertainty to clarity, from self-doubt to self-assuredness, and from confusion to purpose. It offers a personalised and supportive environment to explore our true selves, set meaningful goals, and take proactive steps towards a more fulfilling life. We can unlock our full potential and create positive change in our lives and the world around us.

Maybe you are exploring becoming a coach. I invite you to challenge your own misconceptions about what it is and how it differs from modalities like counselling or mentoring. Do so with an open mind, be curious and try things even if they feel unnatural at the beginning.

The thing to note is that it doesn't have to be an either-or situation: coaching fits in a range of situations and pretty much any topic imaginable. It has a utility one-on-one but is also an effective tool to support and develop teams.

As you learn more about coaching you will start to see pockets of coaching techniques in interactions everywhere from teachers and work colleagues to friends. Perhaps they don't recognise it as coaching but think about those times you've experienced someone really listening, really hearing you, saying little but asking questions that somehow get to the root of the problem and you think of a solution without them telling you what the answer is.

I invite you to embrace coaching. Whether you are contemplating becoming a coach or simply looking to benefit from coaching's life-changing potential. When you do open yourself up to it, it's an environment of inclusivity, accessibility, and empowerment where you can transcend conventional stereotypes and eradicate any stigma associated with self-improvement.

If you've ever considered embracing coaching, let this be your call to action, your invitation to join a community of fellow explorers on a remarkable journey. Together, we can illuminate the world with the profound power of coaching. Take this from a middle-aged man who misunderstood it for way too long.

ABOUT ADAM CENEY

Adam Ceney is an accredited career coach who helps people at the mid-point of their careers bring clarity to their thinking so they can find their unique value and create the freedom to have a career compatible with the life they have or want on their terms.

As well as a coach, Adam has been a management consultant for over ten years specialising in data and analytics within the UK public sector. He has worked in a range of organisations from large corporates to start-ups and now coaches and mentors people to navigate their career options and create opportunities that work for them.

Adam enjoys writing, making music, and coaching his son's football team.

Adam is available for coaching, mentoring as well as private consultations.

You can reach Adam at:

Email: adam@createimpactcoaching.com

linkedin.com/in/adamceney

3

"THE BIGGEST BARRIER TO MY SUCCESS IS MYSELF" — ADNAN ALI

There is no greater satisfaction than seeing and hearing the moment a person begins to become aware of who they are, why they are the way they are, and what causes them to do what they do. Becoming aware is a pivotal moment in a person's coaching journey, and only after this can that person take the necessary action to make a change.

Awareness can come in multiple forms. It can be awareness of how added sugar in food can eventually be stored as fat. It can be awareness of how our own behaviours impact on relationships with others. It can be awareness of how our childhood experiences have moulded our adult lives. It can be awareness of how our feelings manifest as physical sensations. Once we become aware, we can then make an informed decision on the actions we do, or do not, want to take.

Whether you are training for a marathon, studying a course or progressing in your career, awareness is a tool that can excel your progress. Let's look at the example of training for a marathon. A runner needs to be aware of their current physical ability, their current endurance, and their current performance. By knowing these factors, they will have a good starting point from which to implement a training program. A more successful runner will also be aware of what is required from them in terms of time commitment and nutrition. Being aware of how their day-to-day life, work, family, social and other commitments affect their ability to stick to a schedule will also improve their chances of success. Being aware of how they trained for previous attempts at completing a marathon, or any challenge, will allow them to look for learnings and implement those into their training program.

In the same manner, any person wanting to overcome a challenge or make an improvement to themselves can utilise the power of awareness. The process of becoming aware requires honesty, inward reflection, and acceptance. A coach who can listen, ask timely questions and be curious can enable this. Along with offering constructive feedback, the accountability a coach can provide can also enable the person to transform their increased awareness into actions that allow them to make the maximum impact on themselves and others.

As I sat waiting to start my coaching session, I reflected on how I had got here. As with every coaching session, the coach would soon be asking me what I wanted to talk about. It was now or never – should I talk about the thing that was really on my mind? I didn't feel restless or agitated, nor did I feel on edge. My heart wasn't racing, and my palms were not sweaty. I did however have a certain sense of something intangible and difficult to put into words at the time, a feeling of unease. It was the feeling you get when you're about to do a bungee jump. You know that you're going to be safe, you know that if you never do it, you will never have challenged yourself and will always be wondering "what if", but there's still that niggle, that risk that it could all go wrong. It's the feeling of dread that occurs when you step out of your comfort zone, just as I was debating whether to do during this session.

Previous experiences with coaching had always seemed superficial but I knew this was because I was holding back. I realised that I was only going to benefit by being open and trusting. I had to trust that the coach was not going to judge me or belittle my thoughts and I also had to trust in the process.

So, I made the decision that day that I would be truly open. And what happened was amazing.

Since my early teens, I had struggled to meet deadlines, more often than not either not completing something or leaving a task to the last minute.

I would sign up for challenges and then not properly trained for them. I would turn up at the starting line having fought off intrusive thoughts of what excuse I could give for not being able to take part, or whether I could feign injury or turn up late and miss the whistle. During the actual event, I would struggle physically and mentally, unable to keep up with peers, unable to visualise reaching the finish line, and usually having to walk vast sections.

I would leave educational assignments to the last minute. Whether this was at university, whilst training to be a GP, or completing additional training, I would always leave the completion of my assignments to the very end, pulling all-nighters, and knowing that I had never actually submitted work to the best of my potential or ability.

More recently, I recorded podcast interviews that I had not published. This was directly impacting my profile and my business and was not fair to those who had kindly given up their time to share their stories with me.

The stress and anxiety associated with then finding the time to complete and submit the task would take over. I would eat sugary biscuits and snacks, sleep fewer hours, and stop going to the gym. It impacted not only my health, sleep and eating habits but also those of the people around me, including family and friends who would be at the sharp edge of my emotions.

I didn't know why I would not complete things, or why I would leave them to the last minute, but I knew that for me to develop, I had to do something about it. I had tried to manage my diary better, I had tried to plan, I had tried to make changes to my environment, but ultimately, I would find myself back in the same place.

It wasn't easy but I decided there and then, in that day's session, I would focus on how I could get tasks completed, and ahead of time. Andrew's approach was relaxed and calming and after our usual pleasantries he asked, "What would I like to talk about today?" Usually, I would um and ah as I would never have prepared for a coaching session, but that day I knew exactly what my reply was going to be. "I want to be able to complete the things I start."

I expected that Andrew would ask me a few questions, I would give some suitable answers, and then we would move on to coming up with some options and actions and come to the end of our session. I was wrong. In that session, I realised that my perception of poor timekeeping being the cause was just at the surface, and in fact, there were deeper, more sub-conscious causes that I had to address.

The power of coaching is in peeling away the layers to get to the root of the reality behind the issue. The technique for doing so is by asking good questions, and the science behind asking good questions is to listen and hold space. The best questions are not the ones that have been pre-formulated but are the ones that come naturally due to a cue or particular phrase a client said. Andrew was brilliant at this. Our session started with Andrew asking questions to explore what I wanted to complete, whether there was a specific example and what I wanted to achieve in the session. I talked about editing and publishing a podcast interview I had recently done. Rather than immediately trying to work out what I could do to publish the podcast, Andrew utilised his questioning skills to probe further into what was behind the procrastination.

"What is it about publishing the podcast that makes you hesitate?"

This was the question that stopped me in my tracks. I felt myself take in a deep breath and realised this was the moment where I could resist or allow the layers to be peeled. I could allow myself to be open and therefore have the opportunity to progress, or I could resist and remain stuck in my ways.

"I'm scared that people will not like it."

This was the moment of change. This was the moment of realisation. This was the moment I had truly been honest to myself and expressed the reason behind the last-minute assignments, the incompleted tasks and the late-night stress. This was the moment I was beginning to become aware of myself.

But the thing is, this may seem like some sort of "ah-ha!" moment, but it wasn't. I knew all along, deep down, that the reason was based on fear, but by expressing and verbalising it, I was able to acknowledge its presence. Awareness is what comes next.

Rather than reacting in a diagnostic manner and saying to me "There you go, that's your problem", Andrew was able to hold the space and make great use of silence to allow me to further express what was going through my mind. Very often, coaches are quick to move on. This becomes coach-centric rather than coachee-centric. By holding the space, I was able to talk through what made me think this.

Andrew held the space, using a mixture of silence and questions. The questions were not pre-considered; they were based on my responses. For instance, one of the questions that came out was, "What previous experience have you had where a piece of work resulted in a negative reaction, and what did that mean for me?" Hearing this question, my mind travelled back to pivotal moments in my life. I thought about the time a teacher advised me that applying to study medicine was not for me, I would never get in and should choose an alternative subject. I thought about the time I opened a restaurant and a colleague mockingly questioned whether they would get food poisoning by eating there. I thought about the time an employer had questioned me sharing my successes on social media as this displayed a form of arrogance. I wasn't sure whether I wanted to re-live these experiences now, in this session.

Reflecting on my initial resistance, I found myself grappling with the fear of being judged by the coach. What would the coach think if I revealed what I was truly thinking? This emphasises the importance of coaching agreements, confidentiality, and the need to work with a properly trained and accredited professional.

Navigating this resistance was challenging. There was an internal struggle between my desire to talk about my concerns and the fear of judgment. Eventually, I decided to trust the process and allowed myself to be open. This internal shift marked a turning point in the session.

By sharing, I was able to learn that these experiences were not a reflection on me. I had gained entry to medical school, I had run a successful restaurant, and my successes were exactly that – successes, and there was no arrogance in sharing them. As it happens, I had allowed these experiences to compound, and then become reinforced when I did not complete something. By accepting that these were not a reflection of my abilities, I was able to move forward.

The pivotal moment occurred when I realised that my fear was the root cause of my procrastination. Expressing it out loud made me confront the irrationality of this fear. Why should the opinions of others work be a barrier for me?

This realisation brought a sense of relief. It was like a weight had been lifted off my shoulders. The fear that had held me back for so long suddenly seemed trivial and baseless. I felt a sense of excitement and renewed vigour.

Acknowledging this fear changed my perspective entirely. I was no longer worried about how others perceived my work. Instead, I focused on putting my work out there, accepting feedback and using it constructively. This shift empowered me, making me feel more in control of my actions and decisions.

In the end, this transformation not only changed my perception of my abilities but also made me more comfortable with self-expression. I began to openly share my beliefs, mission, values, and goals, not just for the sake of sharing, but as a way to hold myself accountable and inspire others through my experiences.

Having worked through the initial part of the coaching session, it was now important to ensure there was a good set of actionable steps. These actions needed to be because of the insights that had been gained to ensure the maximum chance of implementation. Too many times, we express our inner thoughts and feelings but then do not allow these to translate into actions that take these into account.

In medicine, we have a concept of informed decision-making, which is also an integral aspect of the Mental Capacity Act. Informed decision-making is based on being aware of the thoughts behind a particular issue, and then taking actions based on that awareness. A similar concept can be applied to ensuring actions are also informed. As a result, such actions are less reactive and more empowering to personal growth.

Andrew's coaching style was facilitative and challenging at the same time, to reinforce the insights. It was facilitative in that I produced a list of next steps that would allow me to move forward but also challenging in that I reviewed past actions that were not in keeping with the insights I had gained. Previously, when I had tried to tackle similar difficulties with completing and finishing tasks, I had taken arbitrary steps such as blocking out time in my calendar, but then not sticking to it. It was important to tailor strategies to ensure my actions weren't one-size-fits-all, but bespoke solutions, maximising their effectiveness and making my progress more profound and sustainable.

I had to think outside of the box to avoid making the same mistakes and embrace methods that I had previously not tried such as keeping a journal to express my thoughts and feelings, using accountability partners, and mapping out work ahead of time.

Most importantly, I had to practice gratitude. Gratitude spiritually, inwardly, and outwardly. Gratitude for the abilities I had been given and been blessed with. Gratitude for opportunities and challenges and life's ups and downs. Gratitude allows one to shift perspective from negativity to positivity. Gratitude improves resilience. Gratitude enhances self-esteem.

As a result of my coaching experiences, I'm no longer held back and believe I have managed to make decisions that have allowed me to change my focus to the career that I want to focus on. I am creating more and I'm more willing to share my experiences openly. Writing this book chapter is a huge challenge for me, yet here I am!

My biggest success has been the feedback from other people. When you learn to cut out the negativity and learn to cut out the negative thoughts, you can focus on the positives. When somebody tells you that something you have written or something that you've said has inspired them to make a change, it brings a sense of real satisfaction, a real sense of achievement, and you realise you're making an impact and that in turn, pushes you along.

Going through coaching allowed me to express, tackle and work through challenges that I would otherwise have ignored. As it turns out, there's a lot more to life that affects you.

Through my experiences, I've developed my unique coaching style, based around awareness. I have developed the AWARE model of coaching, which is a set of steps that a person can use themselves or be guided through:

Acknowledging their feelings,
being **W**illing to be open,
Accepting their feelings and thoughts,
Reflecting and then,
being **E**mpowered to move on.

HOW TO USE THE AWARE COACHING MODEL

Trying to work through our emotions and understanding the many layers of our thoughts is like embarking on an expedition with ourselves. The AWARE Model provides a structured approach to peeling away the layers. This model delves into five fundamental pillars: Acknowledge, Willingness, Acceptance, Reflection and Empowerment.

Acknowledge:

The model commences with acknowledging our emotions – the flags of our inner state. It's about recognising the subtleties of our feelings, understanding their origins, and accepting them without judgment. When we acknowledge our emotions, we grant them validation, granting ourselves the freedom to explore their depths. This process involves peeling back the layers and delving into the core of our sentiments, whether they be fear, joy, or uncertainty.

Some questions to consider could be:

- What emotions am I feeling right now and where do I think they stem from?
- Are there any recurring patterns in my emotional responses to specific situations or people?
- How comfortable am I with acknowledging my vulnerabilities and fears? What steps can I take to become more accepting of them?

Willingness:

The next step is willingness – the readiness to be vulnerable, to open our thoughts and feelings. It's about embracing the discomfort that often accompanies self-exploration. Willingness is the bridge between acknowledging our emotions and accepting them. It's the ability to confront our fears, the courage to face our uncertainties and the resilience to withstand the challenges of our inner turmoil.

Some questions to consider could be:

- Am I willing to confront my fears and step out of my comfort zone to achieve my goals?
- What limiting beliefs or self-doubts am I willing to let go of in order to progress?
- In what areas of my life am I resistant to change and how can I cultivate a willingness to embrace transformation?

Acceptance:

Acceptance is the cornerstone of the AWARE model - embracing ourselves entirely, flaws, insecurities, and all. It involves making peace with our past, acknowledging the scars that have shaped us, and understanding that they are symbols of our resilience. Acceptance releases us from the thoughts of self-criticism, allowing us to embrace our imperfections.

Some questions to consider could be:

- What aspects of myself do I struggle to accept and why?
- How can I reframe my perceived flaws as unique qualities that make me who I am?
- What past experiences am I finding it challenging to accept and how can I work towards forgiveness and closure?

Reflection:

This is where we delve into the depths of our experiences, extracting invaluable lessons from our past. It's a process of looking inwards and an examination of our actions, reactions, and decisions. Through reflection, we gain clarity, revealing patterns that have shaped our thoughts.

Some questions to consider could be:

- What recurring patterns or behaviours have I noticed in my past actions and decisions?
- How have my past experiences shaped my current beliefs and values?

- What valuable lessons have I learned from my past mistakes and how can I apply them to my future endeavors?

Empowerment:

The peak of the AWARE coaching model culminates in empowerment. It's not just about understanding ourselves; it's about harnessing this knowledge to drive change. Empowerment is the conscious decision to rewrite our narrative, transform our weaknesses into strengths and move our fears towards progress. It's about taking everything into consideration to maximise chances of success.

Some questions to consider could be:

- What specific actions can I take today to empower myself and move closer to my goals?
- In what ways can I use my strengths and talents to make a positive impact on my life and the lives of others?
- What self-care practices can I incorporate into my routine to nurture my physical, mental, and emotional well-being, fostering a sense of empowerment?

The AWARE coaching model has enabled me to help numerous clients. Here are just a few examples:

Case One

One of the most powerful comments from a client, having been through this, was "The biggest barrier to my success is myself". This was a client who had been in a role for a particularly long time and had never really progressed. She had never really tried challenging herself.

Sarah had remained sitting in the back thinking that she wasn't quite good enough and therefore, she never really pushed herself. It was only when she started going through the coaching process that she started thinking outside the box.

She stepped outside of her comfort zone and talked about things that were uncomfortable. She accepted those feelings and then reflected on what could be done to challenge those thoughts, and then moved on to empowerment. Sarah worked in a corporate role, in a small team and never thought that she would be able to move into a more senior management role. She had a persistent feeling of inadequacy and a belief that she wasn't capable of taking on such a position. Her fear was such that she would not even apply for a role internally, as that would mean attending an interview and having to talk about herself and (in her mind) being exposed as someone who was not even good at the role she was doing.

Eventually, she realised that she was being held back, not just by others, but by herself. She wasn't deliberately sabotaging herself, but she was also not taking the steps to change or grow herself and was very uncomfortable with it inside. She realised that this was not what she wanted to be doing. Accepting this involved acknowledging deep-seated fears of failure and rejection. Overcoming this required small and consistent actions to test these thought processes. Sarah's willingness to be open and try new approaches allowed her to learn and develop her confidence in herself.

Case Two

Many people want to live a healthier life, lose weight and exercise more. They have great intentions and start diet plans and exercise programs with vigour and enthusiasm, but frequently, this drive is short-lived. The programs fall by the wayside and the person returns to their previous way of living. Those who do continue and persist are the ones who have a holistic awareness of their life.

Simon had health issues and had tried multiple ways of improving his diet or losing weight but was never successful. On occasion, he had managed to achieve some weight loss but never managed to keep the weight off. Simon was frustrated with his experiences and felt that he would never be able to live the healthy life he desired. It became apparent very quickly that Simon's challenges were more than not eating well or exercising and in fact, his work, and the stress that he experienced, played a significant part. He had been setting himself up for failure by not acknowledging the stress and not doing anything about it, which meant that when things were not going right, he was going back to old habits very quickly.

Confronting and accepting the impact of work on his lifestyle was pivotal for Simon. By being more aware of this, he was able to make informed decisions about what he wanted to do, and he decided to leave his role and take up a position abroad, which is something he always wanted to do. Leaving his role had a profound positive impact, with improved physical and mental health, and better work-life balance.

Case Three

Carole is a very confident individual who wanted to make a difference through her business but was struggling with promoting herself. Carole's outgoing persona was confident and charismatic, but she was hesitant to showcase her work through social media or workshops and constantly worried that nobody would be interested in her work.

Acknowledging that she wanted to work through challenges that were holding her back, and her willingness to be open allowed her to realise that imposter syndrome was holding her back from posting on social media. Through coaching, Carole came to realise that there was a disconnect between her capabilities and that her inadequacies were perceived. The awareness that this was imposter syndrome allowed Carole to move forward.

Recognising triggers, re-framing negative thoughts and celebrating achievements became useful parts of her toolkit as she worked through small actions. This shift in mindset empowered her to promote herself and her business confidently and make the impact that she was hoping to make.

As you can see, being aware of how your emotions, feelings, thoughts, previous experiences, and beliefs impact you can have a profound effect on your growth and future success.

> "Believe in yourself and all that you are. Know that there is something inside you that is greater than any obstacle."
>
> — CHRISTIAN D. LARSON

ABOUT ADNAN ALI

Dr. Adnan Ali is a GP and accredited coach who helps individuals and organisations to develop and maintain positive habits that impact their life and health, and that of their people.

Before launching Open Box Coaching, Adnan worked as an NHS GP and a medical leader for 12 years. After a successful career helping individuals from all backgrounds manage their health problems and training aspiring leaders and managers, Adnan now coaches individuals and businesses by taking a holistic approach to health and wellbeing.

Adnan loves the mountains having climbed all the major peaks in the Lake District. In the summer, he enjoys camping trips with his family and friends. Recently he has taken up golf and is working on getting his handicap to single figures.

Adnan is available for coaching, training and private consultations.

You can reach Adnan at:

Email: adnan@openboxcoaching.com
Website: www.openboxcoaching.com

facebook.com/dradnanalimrcgp
linkedin.com/in/dradnanali

4

FINDING THE COURAGE TO BE YOURSELF: HOW COACHING CAN HELP EMPOWER THOSE WITH ADHD TO OVERCOME SYMPTOMS AND FLOURISH — ANNA BADCOCK

COACHING'S POTENTIAL TO ACT AS A TRIAGE FACILITY TO DETERMINE WHETHER MEDICATION IS NECESSARY TO MANAGE THE CONDITION

"It's knowing I'm not alone. I'm not mad. I'm not unlovable. I'm not depressed. I'm not rubbish. I'm not controlling." Her eyes glistened in the Zoom room as the words tumbled out. "I'm not different."

"Being part of this group has changed my life. So many people need to hear this message. They need to have this knowledge and information. They need to be part of a trusting group like this. All that is 'different' about me is that I have ADHD, as does everyone here – which makes me not so very different at all."

The soft, warm wind rustled the leaves outside and the dogs snored contentedly beside me. A seismic, energetic shift had happened in the digital room. Everyone was united - nodding, empathising, agreeing.

The group had come together to road test *The HyperFocus Method* Coaching programme I had developed for people with ADHD. Plenty of people in my network identified as having ADHD, thought they had it, or had a recent diagnosis - so I'd bent a few elbows and persuaded them to join me on this beta test journey.

When my own children were diagnosed, I did my research on support for ADHD and found there were plenty of apps for ADHD, some ADHD specialist coaches, and the odd group coaching session. I also knew there wasn't anything available in the mould of what I was looking at delivering.

I had absolute belief that what I was offering would change people's lives in positive ways – better organisation, accountability to take action, and self-knowledge about why their brains worked the way they did. Neither they nor I were prepared for the outcome that transpired.

"I'd always felt like the white rabbit in *Alice in Wonderland*. Always late, always flustered, feeling very alone in this inability to be organised, on top of things and in control. Thinking I was the unique failure."

She averted her eyes, cast them down, drew breath. "I've done a lot of coaching and learning online, but for the first time, I feel a meeting of minds in this group. I haven't had to change to fit in. I could – possibly for the first time – just be me."

Belonging is such a fundamental requirement to life that Maslow placed it right at the heart of his famous Hierarchy of Needs, straight after the food, shelter and safety we must have to live.

The HyperFocus Method™ hadn't just delivered knowledge, coaching, organisational tactics, emotional regulation strategies, or wellbeing goals. By bringing them together in a unique way, with proper trust, support and engagement, as a bunch of people who all had the same kind of mind, we'd delivered something much more important.

We had provided a space where they could let the mask slip and be comfortable. They could know they were understood within a community of like-minded souls to whom they could turn and be honest about their darkest days.

We had fundamentally changed lives by helping people find the courage to be themselves.

IT WASN'T ALWAYS THIS WAY

The world had shut down and I was lying in bed, a victim. Floored by some post-Covid fatigue that was un-nameable yet unstinting in its debilitation.

Liza Minelli mightn't be the first person you'd think of in a crisis, but as I stared at the ceiling, my saviour appeared. Years ago, describing how she'd recovered from injury to return to the world stage, Liza said to her interviewer, "I couldn't do much in that state, but I knew I wasn't done. I thought about what I could do. And after all the years I'd spent in rehearsal, I knew I could practice. So, every day I practiced how to walk again. Little by little. Step by step. And as I practised, I grew stronger. At first, I could only stand still. Then I could walk tentatively, then confidently. And then I could dance."

What could I do? I was a long way from dancing, and regardless, the musical theatre stage had never had me in its sights.

But I could read, and I could learn.

Throughout life, whenever I was in a disorientating situation, I'd always pick up a book. Held in solitary in the Middle East by border guards – a book. Stuck on a train platform in Eastern Europe immediately after Glasnost – a book. Up a mountain in Nepal with thunderous avalanches echoing around me – a book.

But learning doesn't just happen in books – you often have to turn up in a classroom too. I'd been about to study to increase my digital marketing knowledge for a job, but the course I'd signed up for kicked off with an in-person event and had been postponed.

Was there a course I could do from my bed? The worldwide shutdown possibly had an upside.

Tap, tap on the iPad. Up popped a few. One started with a free two-week learning challenge for an hour a day. Online. Bingo. I signed up in seconds.

Day one: introductions and a group session with the resident life coach.

Forget Liza's wisdom. Even propped up with pillows, withered and exhausted as I was, like a thunderbolt, anything and everything seemed possible. All I needed to change was my mind.

My memory was stirred to recall the exchange I'd had with a life coach during a PR gig years ago. When she had explained how coaching worked, I'd felt the gut lurch you get when you lock eyes across a room with someone who sees into your soul.

And here it was again whilst I was studying something else. It felt like a betrayal akin to an affair. Here I was wedded to one area of study and into the bar sauntered the dashing, dangerous 'other'.

Life in that bed was mighty dull, and the stranger of coaching was intoxicating.

Tap, tap on the iPad. Another free learning challenge, this time for Neuro Linguistic Programming (NLP) and Life Coaching. I clicked, I saw, I signed up.

And so, the affair started. It was a dance between improving my marketing skills by day and in the shadows going deeper and deeper into Coaching. That universe kept calling me. First with whispers, glances. Then one day, inescapably.

"I am gifting you this course at the lowest price I can offer, because I know you must do this. I know this is the right step for you," said one mentor.

And then the friend who had sat beside me in school and stood beside me through life took the step with me. She endorsed my choice. She agreed. We both made the leap into the 'proper', rigorous, industry-leading ICF course. For the first time in decades, we were back in the classroom together.

My fling with Coaching, having hidden in plain sight for months, claiming it was just the support act to my 'real' job, was suddenly outed. I had no intention of staying committed to marketing, and it was obvious to everyone.

My husband, ever astute, wasn't the least bit surprised, but was exasperated. Would my perpetual learning renaissance ever end? Would it ever grow into a committed job?

What was the goal?

I didn't dare say the truth – that I wasn't sure what success looked like for me and what the future held. But when I emerged from that bed in lockdown, and gathered strength and finally engaged in family life again, the future presented itself before my eyes.

With three teenage boys, lockdown had felt like a university flat share with the rugby team: messy, food-orientated, back-to-back media consumption, a pressing need for regular exercise, and the odd nod to academia.

It was in one of those academic sessions with my middle son, during which we navigated excruciating online exams (I was both reader and scribe to his dyslexic needs) that it was no longer an option to ignore the possibility he may have ADHD.

I sat beside him like a 1950s secretary and diligently typed his every thought, while he did spectacular somersaults in his chair, frequently answering questions about *Macbeth* whilst standing on his head.

I, like many parents up and down the land and around the globe, could barely believe my child was able to take in anything at all whilst being so monumentally distracted by his own brain and body. It was nothing short of a miracle that he'd absorbed even the slightest knowledge of the Battle of Hastings or a times table.

I had finally found the right support for his dyslexia after spending years battling. Not for the first time, I was awash with gratitude and admiration for his teachers. But he was about to leave and start senior school. I became convinced we'd be out by Christmas unless I acted on finding a diagnosis, help and support for his ADHD.

But one night, in the depths of lockdown, it suddenly felt like it might be too late.

After watching a movie, he uncharacteristically became traumatised by it. He was inconsolable and terrified, unable to even close his eyes. Sleep was impossible night after night. He slept beside my bed on an assembled collection of duvets and blankets. The images replayed in his mind, each time more real and more terrifying. Trapped in the house, with no friends or change of environment to distract him, the replay was endless.

On night three, I decided to try a recently learned NLP technique, and he and I quietly and calmly did it together, changing his thought process, and reprogramming his brain. It worked. He and I slept solidly side by side for the first time in days, hands touching.

Riddled with worry for my child, I thought, *I cannot be alone in this. There must be others.*

There were others – right upstairs as it turned out.

"I think I've got it too."

"No – you're not! You're not jumping on the bandwagon. Annoying as this is, your brother needs more attention from me, and this is no way to get more for yourself."

"No really, Mum. Please listen. I absolutely think I have ADHD too. I did test after test online. They all say I do."

I listened. He was right. He had just been really, really good at hiding it.

During lockdown, distractions ceased to exist. Coping strategies belonging to the dusty desks of schools and workplaces disappeared. Friends vanished into the ether of the screen.

There were others. Thousands and thousands of others would emerge from this lockdown knowing they couldn't ignore their symptoms any longer. Life wasn't manageable without the strategies honed through a life lived behind a mask and the symptoms shouted too loudly to be ignored. The mask had slipped.

Like in all seismic shifts, there were the deniers who refused to believe that the plates of change had unearthed a truth that had been hiding in plain sight.

"I've found it," I said to that mentor who had begged me to do the coaching course with her. "I have finally found what I should be coaching. My children have ADHD; it is pretty likely that my husband and I have it too. From the bits of coaching I've done with students and clients who have ADHD, I'm convinced that coaching can help manage and alleviate symptoms with or without medication."

"I can tell this comes from your heart," she said, "and you have to do this."

GETTING THERE

I love getting the big, fat badge that proves I can do something, so as I set off on my coaching journey, I made sure I'd covered all the badge bases.

There were many people claiming to be coaches who were really teachers, trainers or consultants. Brilliant at what they did, but not coaches in the true sense. If I was going to stand up as a coach, I wanted to make sure I could be what I was claiming to be.

Everyone I learned from was the best at what they did. I learned great tactics, knowledge, theory, and academic study about many parts of coaching from NLP to Positive Psychology. I also wanted the industry-leading ICF badge and registration so did my research and found Optimus, which appealed to me with its inclusion of Positive Psychology and Neuroscience, mentoring and flexible hours, plus long-term support.

A learning timetable began that would make most people weep, doing two, three or four courses in tandem (classic ADHD behaviour), as well as working.

As with all rigorous study, each course took months, and it took years to do everything I wanted to, even burning the weekend oil. I was also committed to several jobs, so I planned a timetable of stepping back over nearly two years.

I also knew I had to practise what I was to preach. I received more hours of coaching and mentoring than I was delivering to others. Sometimes the pace of it all became unsustainable.

I listened to advice on how to grow a business and brought in people and systems early on – long before most people would – because I knew my ADHD needed it. Without support, overwhelm and procrastination would have dominated, and I would have gone in ever-expanding learning circles without any progression to delivery (just as my husband feared).

I paid attention to my strengths and weaknesses, was brutally honest with myself about my weak areas and identifying the mind blocks that got in the way of finding solutions.

My learning curve was more a march up a steeply-sided mountain at double speed. I drew on every life experience that had ever taught me resilience, from marathon running and yomping over hills to having three children under the age of four to managing jobs and family whilst poleaxed with grief. I walked my dogs early each day and partied with friends at weekends to keep me happy.

But not everyone loved this version of me.

I had to ditch the mid-week activities I'd picked up through the years of toddler groups and school gates. Some bemoaned that I was never available for leisurely dog walks, lunches or any new time-filling activities now the children were growing up. Some just stopped calling. Some ridiculed my ambition. Some pretended they were unavailable when I was free, point-scoring rejection touchés.

I had always been busy, often juggling two or three jobs. But I had always found time to maintain the daytime socials through rigorous diary management and determination. I enjoyed them.

But lockdown had stripped those away and forced me to find a replacement. I had, and now that seductive affair with coaching, which had flourished whilst we had all been shut away, was fully uncovered and the implications on my time exposed.

I could no longer hide this passion and the consequences were stark.

Fortunately, many more were supportive and encouraging. Others were grateful – what could I share that they needed support with too? And finally, some sat up, engaged, intrigued. They wanted to be involved. They said yes to being part of test groups. They made the most of my cheaper training rates. They became my best, most committed clients and remain so.

One such person opened my eyes to the need for ADHD coaching around the same time as I was working with my children's schools to help their teachers understand the specific needs of the ADHD child.

"I know what I am supposed to be doing, and I really want to do everything we discuss in our sessions. I am desperate to move forward and take action, but I'm exhausted and my life is so different from one day to the next that I can't seem to find any consistency. I'm so sorry, I think I must be a terrible person to coach," she said.

We explored several ways she might get more rest or support, and over several weeks used the coaching tools, techniques and strategies which were to form the basis of *The HyperFocus Method*™. A unique set of circumstances for this client meant it was easy to find reasons why she would find action hard, but despite this, she was able to make some changes and take small steps.

One step included talking this through with her doctor, after which he suggested ADHD medication. For the first time, coaching had helped as a triage tool. It was also her saviour post-diagnosis and post-medication, helping her find ways of behaving with her newfound ability to concentrate that rocket-fuelled her progress.

"Is this a real or a thought-based problem?" I asked another client during a coaching session. They had a difficult home life, and we were trying to sift the thoughts and fears from reality.

It was a problem I knew well, having had to ask myself the same question many times over the past few months and years. The answer provides the start of figuring out the solution – what needs to change? Do we start with practicalities or mindset?

Bringing up three children all with dyslexia and ADHD, navigating the teenage years, GCSEs, and A Levels, all in the long shadow of the consequences of lockdown, managing aging parents, running a home, whilst starting a career and business from scratch was never going to a walk in the park. But there was no Plan B. It had to work because of my family, because of my intense connection with coaching and positive psychology. My family needed this knowledge of how to navigate ADHD and flourish with it. They have been my learning model, my purpose.

Since those dark nights lying awake with my son as his mind raced and I held his hand to comfort him to sleep, I knew there had to be a better way. What if this happened when I wasn't there? How many others were not so lucky to have found that magic tactic that saved us? What happened to them?

DELIVERY

What happened to them became clear as I started my research into the ADHD world. I joined and engaged in groups, read book after book, and followed leading figures in the ADHD world.

Some were desolate about how they could manage life at all when every part of life proved a challenge, from getting out of bed to deciding what to eat. Some were high performers, super successful but hanging on by a thread to 'looking normal'. Many had been diagnosed with depression for years before enlightened psychiatrists realised it was probably ADHD instead.

Every type of person was represented in the forums, groups and people I followed. There was no 'typical' version although there were plenty of common symptoms. When people talked about their experiences, others were staggered that their quirks and traits were shared, and they were not alone.

The common thread amongst a group of people for whom every single diagnosis and presentation of the condition was different was that they felt alone in their suffering and that their only respite and salvation was through medication.

It also became clear, as was the case with our family, that no one version was the same as another.

As I researched and learned more about ADHD, I benefited hugely from a very open community. Until very recently, ADHD was largely thought of as something 'naughty boys' had. Even now, many defer from diagnosis in fear of a label that will deem them unemployable and difficult.

But such is the tidal wave of diagnosis, and the bravery of some very high-profile people sharing their story, that the lightbulb of recognition has been lit for many others. Women and girls have realised they can have it too, and ironically, this has also helped more boys to be honest and courageous about their diagnosis as the stigma around the 'naughty boys' label starts to fall away.

My training to become a Positive Psychology Coach had taught me that there was more to the mind than many of us had begun to consider, and I was struck by how many of the techniques, tools and practices I had learned in Neuro-Linguistic Programming, Positive Psychology, Neuroscience and via the International Coach Federation training could be applied to help and support the ADHD mind specifically.

It struck me that ADHD can't be fixed with a one-off blast of medication, coaching or anything else. Yet after the cost that many need to pay for a private diagnosis, the extra cost of one-to-one coaching with no end in sight feels out of reach and insurmountable.

I started volunteering as a coach for ADHD UK, which offers one-off coaching for free to members, and some people also use the UK Government's Access to Work scheme which offers six free coaching sessions for ADHD. But a short burst of coaching would have the same impact a short course of medication might – helpful while it happens, but not the long-term solution ADHD needs.

As ADHD is a difference in the wiring of the brain, it occurred to me that an approach similar to treating eyesight differences would help. A course of treatment for eyesight or a pair of glasses that only lasted for six weeks would be little help. A long-term solution was found for correcting eyesight –we need to update it regularly (glasses or contact lenses), but it helps us live a normal life.

I thought an approach to ADHD that offered a complement to medication with different cost options could prove successful, in much the same way we might choose to use both contact lenses and glasses.

I knew the greatest gift of this programme needed to be a life-long toolkit of self-care, knowledge and tactics that clients could use time and time again to bring them back on track if they ever felt their ADHD symptoms spiralling out of control, plus a community that could support each other.

I led some 'Everyday ADHD' coaching sessions with ADHD UK, with the numbers joining improving each month. I offered knowledge and insight about how the brain works (ADHD people love to know the 'why' of things before they act), and tactics to help with everyday problems such as lost keys and time blindness. People who had joined the sessions started contacting me and recommending me to other friends.

I set up a beta test version of a methodology I had created specifically for ADHD.

Several people on my client list were perfect candidates and they enthusiastically joined. I already knew some had ADHD and had been diagnosed or were going through the diagnosis process. Some confessed to me that they thought they might have it and joined, more to find out if they were right than anything else.

Some thought they didn't have enough time to do it justice. Several were overwhelmed at the thought of a time commitment. Some were sceptical that anything bar drugs could help them.

I listened to them all.

Week one arrived, and we set off with enthusiasm. The information and coaching were structured around supporting the ADHD mind and symptoms, and our assembled crew needed that forgiveness from the neurotypical, linear way these things are usually delivered.

The group quickly settled into trust and vulnerabilities were shared. The intimacy meant they shared and recounted their situations and struggles. Others listened respectfully, enlightened and relieved it wasn't just them with these challenges.

They gained knowledge about why their brains worked as they did, and self-forgiveness followed. They shared survival tactics and explored how they could flourish together. They supported each other as they implemented change.

At the end of our few shared months together, they asked me how this might continue; they wished more people could have this knowledge and support, that so many would be comforted to know they weren't different and alone, just as many of them had felt before we started.

WHAT COMES NEXT?

I had struck gold when I hadn't dared hope that I might even reach bronze. I had learnt the pitfalls and benefits of the offer I had created. I had crafted and recrafted the content and delivery, grateful for feedback and responding to the behaviour of the group.

"Modern life offers no switch-off and that's tough for the ADHD brain to manage," said one. "This has helped me to better manage that overload and avoid burnout. I had seen the use of organisational tools, habits and processes as some form of weakness. *The HyperFocus Method*™ has helped me to see that everyone benefits from these tactics – and that I more than anyone needed them."

At the end of the programme, I asked all the participants to give feedback, and it was unfalteringly positive.

I thought success might look like this and was overwhelmed that I was hitting the goals I'd set out to achieve. I had hoped we might offer a level of support which complemented the medical option of drugs. I didn't anticipate that we could go beyond that.

"I have had literally thousands of hours of therapy, with little impact. If I had left the management of my ADHD to medication, I would have received the dopamine energy and focus to get more jobs done each day, but nothing would have really changed. With *The HyperFocus Method*™ I've gained self-awareness, tactics and strategies, and lost the feelings of failure that used to haunt me and prevent me from taking action. I am now 'better' directly because of your content."

The coaching industry knew it had the strategies and tactics to help with ADHD symptoms, and the plethora of apps designed around this are testament to the possibilities. But as we found through this course, sometimes people need more.

The years of social conditioning that the ADHD brain is 'wrong' can end in guilt, shame and a strong belief amongst those with ADHD that they just aren't good enough. It results in a surfeit of reasons why belief systems emerge, which in turn build walls of safety and prevent people from living a full, happy and thriving life.

The testimonials from the clients who followed *The HyperFocus Method*™ prove that we can reverse that, sometimes with the help of medication and sometimes without it.

People with ADHD may find, whether or not they choose to use medication, that their repeating patterns of behaviour and belief systems can remain. But we can change these; we can break them, challenge and replace them. There is a way forward.

We have found a combination of tactics, tools and strategies that, combined with a strong, supportive and trusting community, mean that our clients have life-changing experiences.

With *The HyperFocus Method*™ they have found that life doesn't have to be a compromise based on how well they can hide their symptoms or structure their lives in secret to support constant burnout possibility or deny themselves the right support because to do so is to 'fail'.

"I allowed my mask to slip in front of this group – I felt safe and trustful. I'm now more comfortable with being 'me' all the time," said one of our clients. "This group is so valuable – I had often felt a 'nutcase' because of my ADHD and I now realise that I'm pretty normal."

So often, we hear people decry ADHD and say that the symptoms that seemingly define it are experienced by everyone. Whilst that might be true, and however hard it is for a neurotypical brain to do something boring like admin, it is ten times harder for the ADHD brain.

Others proclaim that all these people who say they have ADHD must be attention-seeking or so lazy they are looking for excuses not to do anything. Maybe some are.

But imagine failing eyesight was never acknowledged and everyone pretended they could see perfectly so that they weren't ridiculed; then imagine someone invented glasses and contact lenses and the shame around poor vision disappeared. It would suddenly feel like there was an epidemic of eyesight diagnoses, and 'everyone' was wearing glasses.

ADHD can affect how we manage life at every basic level from food prep to everyday organisation; it can impact us as we run businesses and try to keep on top of admin, money and planning; it affects our careers as we try to manage relationships and time management.

If you've got a diagnosis, a hunch of recognition of the symptoms or, like me, you looked at your children's behaviour and saw yourself, then our community is for you.

Many with ADHD have been told and believe that the diagnosis itself will lead to a breakthrough in the symptoms; that once they get the drugs, everything will be okay and they'll operate as normal.

The diagnosis can be monumentally helpful in acceptance of the condition, and the medication improves many of the symptoms, and is life-changing for many.

But medication doesn't teach you strategies and habits to maximise your new ability to manage focus and emotions. It doesn't relieve you of the fears that lie behind the masking of symptoms. It doesn't give you a community of people who fully understand your journey through life.

I think back to that time, late at night, unwell myself and cradling my child, having discovered by chance a way to heal and pledging to help all those who were also awake in the dark.

"The knowledge I gained from *The HyperFocus Method*™ has meant that if and when my ADHD symptoms creep back in, I know why. It's less frightening. I now know that life doesn't have to be hard and there are ways to make life easier that don't equate to failure. I now enjoy being me."

ABOUT ANNA BADCOCK

Anna Badcock is an ADHD, Performance and Wellbeing Coach who helps people with ADHD (Diagnosed; Self Diagnosed; Parents & Carers) to manage symptoms to excel in life, with easy, implementable systems, tactics and behaviour for everyday happiness and success.

Before starting Avita Coaching, Anna spent five years coaching and training Digital Marketing Apprentices many of whom had Dyslexia, ADHD and other educational needs. She also spent over twenty years as a PR and Marketing Consultant and twelve years concurrently as Board Chairman and community leader. Anna has three boys, all of whom have Dyslexia and ADHD.

Anna grew up in the Yorkshire countryside and loves running and walking her dogs outdoors; she loves reading – from biographies to murder mysteries; she is fascinated by Architecture and Interior Design, and can't help but be engaged by Politics and Current Affairs.

You can reach Anna at the following places online and on social media channels. She delivers several ADHD Coaching options – pro bono support, free Facebook groups, Membership and Mastermind groups, and one-to-one Coaching.

Anna also works directly with Business Leaders and Owners on Performance and Wellbeing Coaching.

Email: anna.badcock@avitacoaching.com
Website: https://avitacoaching.com/
Facebook Group: https://www.facebook.com/groups/everydayadhdwithavitacoaching

facebook.com/avitacoach
instagram.com/avitacoaching
linkedin.com/in/annarcfbadcock

5

WHAT EVEN IS 'CAREER FULFILMENT'? — HELEN SCHOEB

Googling 'career fulfilment' gives you various descriptions. Some people define it as having career goals and achieving them; some say it means doing what you enjoy; others point to the knowledge of being in the right job. But what does career fulfilment mean to *you*?

Our versions of career fulfilment are often shaped by our childhood experiences. Consider what you saw and heard as a child concerning work. My own father worked for the same company for fifty years, which is a remarkable achievement. I doubt I will ever again know someone who achieves this, and I'm sure it has shaped my view of loyalty to one's employer. I worked with my first employer for ten years, only leaving when I relocated to London, and then stayed with my new employer for more than ten years.

For me, career fulfilment means looking forward to work, feeling successful and, most importantly, being happy with my career. However, this hasn't always been so clear in my mind, nor has it always been the case during my working life. I particularly remember returning to work once I had young children and feeling like I was on a hamster wheel of work and life. I ended days exhausted, dreaded going to work, and was surviving rather than thriving. I became so busy managing the never-ending to-do lists that there was no time or mental space to reflect on what I was doing and why.

We spend a significant amount of time at work, roughly seventy-five thousand hours on average (based on thirty-five-hour weeks, forty-eight working weeks a year and forty-five years spent working). Shouldn't we all do work we enjoy, have a job we are good at and be happy in our careers?

There are many surveys about what makes people happy at work. Every person within that survey will have their unique perspective of career happiness, just as you have your own version. Maybe earning x amount makes you happy. You might need career development possibilities. You might be happy at work as long as you have the flexibility to pick the kids up from school every day. Or your happiness might depend on having a job with purpose, within a specific industry and with a specific job title.

In 2019, an Investors in People report 'Job exodus trends' showed that sixty-five percent of respondents were happy in their roles - which meant that one in three were unhappy! The report also highlighted that of workers who were seeking new opportunities, thirty percent were looking for more enjoyable work.

Employers should be interested in their employees' happiness and invest in it for many reasons, but especially as evidence suggests that happy workers perform better. An extensive study into happiness and productivity by Said Business School found that workers are thirteen percent more productive when happy. Surely, happiness at work is a win-win situation.

Your happiness at work not only impacts you and your performance but also everyone around you. So, what can you do to have a career you enjoy? I ask a lot of questions as a coach, but you will be pleased to know I also have some answers.

MY FIRST EXPERIENCES OF CAREER COACHING

During my corporate career, I was offered the opportunity for professional development with the Institute of Leadership and Management (ILM) and their Introductory Diploma in Management gave me my first real insight into how different individuals are: perspectives, motivations, strengths, personalities, and natural preferences. I learned how these factors influence people's performance. I learned what drives satisfaction, explored team dynamics, and examined the factors which impact the success of a team.

My self-awareness received a rude awakening. I had to open my eyes to things I had either never thought about, not realised the impact of, or had realised but didn't want to admit to as that might have meant some uncomfortable conversations I didn't want to have.

We had to do the work, we were challenged on our thoughts and opinions, we were listened to (and I mean *really* listened to) and we were coached into becoming better managers. I remain extremely grateful for the opportunity. Whilst I realised at the time that it had made an impact on me, only in hindsight can I fully appreciate the lasting impact it had on me.

At this time I was also introduced to Stephen Covey's book *The Seven Habits of Highly Effective People*. Although some examples and exercises seemed like common sense, I hadn't thought that way before. The saying 'you don't know what you don't know' is very true. I remember being shocked at the simple effectiveness of his circle of concern and circle of influence tool. I often use this model now to ask clients what they can control, what they can influence and what is outside of their control. It is a powerful way to generate new insights, take responsibility and decide on a way forward.

Despite having worked for over a decade and having had experience in managing people and leading teams, it felt like I had just learned on the job and from the guidance of colleagues. I hadn't received any structured training. I hadn't ever had access to coaching. I was promoted because I was good at what I did rather than because I was evidently a good manager or leader. There was no official leadership development programme, just a few away days here and there to encourage collaboration as a senior management team.

I remember specific sessions about performance management and end-of-year appraisals, but nothing to make me stop and think about the type of leader I wanted to be, or even if I wanted to progress my career in that way. There was no investigation of what I wanted and needed to reach my full potential and what would motivate and make me happy. It is common for someone to be a senior member of a corporate team and then move to become the team leader, manager, or director, stepping away from the day-to-day work they excelled in. It is expected that they want to take on a team management role and will excel in this role too, despite the requirement of a completely different set of skills.

I also remember my self-awareness getting another shock when we had a performance coach to help develop our presentation skills. We had to pitch on camera and be critiqued by the coach and colleagues. I would not necessarily recommend this type of coaching for everyone, but it did make me think about what my strengths were. Being recorded on camera was not one of them – although I already knew that. The biggest learning was the exploration into what was behind that belief and what made it so terrifying for me.

We also explored what we can tell from body language, how to engage with people and how to focus on outcomes. We had individual sessions to look at the insights from our presentations and then were coached on the actions we would take away and what support we might need. This coaching intervention made a difference to how I could present in future (which was transactional) but also to what I thought and how I felt about presenting in future (which was transformational).

These coaching experiences gave me insight into how coaching helps with career development, building confidence, overcoming unhelpful thoughts and reframing negative feelings. I saw that self-awareness and mindset were key. I had the insight into how coaching makes a massive difference. Once you have unlocked this insight, what then? What will you do and when?

REASSESSING LIFE

Events in our lives often force us to stop and reassess things. It might be having children, taking on caring responsibilities, facing redundancy, a period of ill health or even enduring a global pandemic. Whatever the reason, changes can offer an excellent time for reflection. There were significant changes in my career after relocating to London and having two children, but the start of school for the children felt like the real turning point. The realisation that my eldest was starting school created a time to stop and consider what was important. Often, a tipping point makes us realise something needs to change. How do we want to spend our time? How do we want to use our energy?

I never had a specific 'dream job' or a defined career goal. There was nothing I felt destined to do from my childhood. No family tradition of careers, no family business, no obvious exceptional talent that was going to make me rich or famous. In the Isle of Man (which I still consider 'home'), many people worked in financial services. It felt like a good place to start and that's what I did.

Over the years, I added professional qualifications, gained promotions and progressed successfully, but I still didn't have in mind a specific role or salary. I was content – or not unhappy, at least – so I carried on doing what I was doing. I felt challenged yet comfortable in my role. I liked the people I worked with. I liked having been at the same place for several years. I liked feeling almost part of the furniture. As the saying goes, 'If it isn't broke don't fix it!' It was a case of *why move?* rather than *why stay?*

When my husband's work took him to London, I decided to relocate with him. Without this catalyst for change, I am not sure if or when I would have left my first employer. I began thinking about who I wanted to work with, and what I would/wouldn't like to do, but in hindsight I was led by recruiters who wanted to place me somewhere that was an easy sell. It turned out to be another great place, with fantastic people and work that provided enough of a push outside my comfort zone but not so much that I wanted to head back 'home'. It was good.

Reflecting on my corporate roles, there were times when I reacted to the opportunities presented to me and times when I took more responsibility for the direction of my career path.

I had always thought, in my ideal world, I would take some time off when the children were young and once they were at school, I would be able to go back to work. Of course, it would be easy once they were at school. I couldn't have been more wrong. I hadn't even done the simple maths with school holidays and work holidays.

Once I had two young children, one in school and bound by school hours, things became much harder to manage. I vividly remember the rush to get kids out of the door on time, the commute to the office, the never-ending to-do-lists, the hurry to get home to see the kids, and logging back on for work in the evenings. And then go again. And again. I started to feel like I wasn't doing enough at work and I wasn't doing enough at home and I was going to end up dead or divorced… and neither of those was good! Something needed to change. I decided it was time to step off the corporate train.

My identity was tied to my corporate career. Losing that was tough. It had been part of my life for over twenty years. I remember meeting other parents after I stopped working and when they asked what I did I would say, 'I'm just a mum.' It didn't take long for me to realise that whilst the corporate career path didn't work at that time, neither was not working.

Every experience teaches us something and we can take lessons from everything. However, this would have been an ideal time for me to invest in a coach!

My time out of the office offered space to reflect on the next path of my career journey. As the employed route no longer felt like the best lifestyle fit, I embarked on life as an entrepreneur. I set up my own online retail business designing and manufacturing children's mini trampolines. A whole different world! It ticked a lot of boxes and I some of my favourite memories are of this time. However, I didn't think through all the implications of what this would mean in terms of the lifestyle that came with it.

There is always an element of not knowing what will happen until you try it. You can only learn so much from reading books, doing courses, and talking to people: you have to just do it. You only really learn from real-life experience.

I again reached a point where that career path no longer worked. I needed to stop and reassess. Yes, there is flexibility in running your own business, but it can seem like there is no off switch. Whilst I had freelance support with PR, social media and outsourced distribution, I was solely responsible for keeping the business going. Solo entrepreneurship can be lonely. I chose to sell the business.

I began to wonder if a corporate career would be better and easier for me or perhaps running a different business would work. Surely there had to be a way to find a fulfilling career without it taking over my life? Then I started thinking about what I had enjoyed throughout my working life so far and what I was good at. I had lots of conversations with friends and family about what I could do next. I was pretty good at knowing all the things I didn't want to do but not so good at knowing what I did want to do.

I noticed key themes. I had the best time in my corporate career because of the people I worked with. The people were what made me want to go to work. In running my own business, I was deeply passionate about the product. I wanted to offer something different and that made a difference. It was also exciting and scary in varying degrees in terms of having to learn new skills. So, people, passion and a commitment to continuous learning…

I started to Google careers and professional development. Lots of searches led me to coaching. Coaching often makes reference to a light bulb moment and this is when I had mine. I found Optimus Coach Academy and joined in with one of their coaching skills weeks. I remember talking to Ruth, the CEO, about the possibility of qualifying as a coach. At that time, I wasn't thinking about coaching as my new career but how coaching skills would be so valuable in life in general. In all honesty, I think I also thought it was a useful excuse not to have to decide anything on the work front for a while because I would be studying instead. Little did I know where this journey would lead.

The Professional Coaching diploma gave us the skills to be ICF accredited coaches. It also included sessions on values, understanding what is important to us, delving into what matters most, and what will motivate and drive us. We considered the extent of our uniqueness and what our talents are. We did strength assessments, personality profiles, exercises like 'be, do, have' in which we visualised what we see ourselves being, doing and having. We covered lots of mindset work to uncover biases and unhelpful limiting beliefs we may have been holding on to. Each of these things was powerful individually but collectively they became self-awareness on steroids. The coaching course also provided access to invaluable mentoring and peer coaching which gave me amazing support and accountability.

My path became clear. Knowing my values and strengths, thinking about how I wanted my career to feature in my life, having a plan, setting goals and having coaching support made me realise what my ideal career could be. In the process of becoming a qualified coach I discovered the formula for career fulfilment. I knew what I needed to be successful and happy in my work. My joy would come from helping others like me find their career fulfilment.

CAREER FULFILMENT COACHING

Once I had identified my next career path and had that 'when you know you know' moment, I realised how passionate I was about helping other people find their own version of career fulfilment in a job they would genuinely enjoy. I realised I wanted to help people look forward to going to work, to be motivated and to maximise their potential. No more just doing the doing, letting time fly by. Too many people are fed up and frustrated at work, wondering *what now, what next*.

Too many people find themselves in jobs they think they should be doing or jobs their partners, parents, peers or even society makes them think they should be doing. I want to support people to step back and invest the time in doing the work to gain the insight they need to determine the right career path for them. Rarely is it the career they think they 'should' have.

While you can discuss your career and next steps with family, friends and colleagues, working with a coach brings a unique perspective. A coach is completely independent, has no vested interest in what you decide to do, no judgement over whether what you are thinking is right or wrong for you, and will get you entirely different results. I know from experience as a coach and coachee that investing in coaching will produce the space to explore options and possibilities and challenge your thinking.

It is common to feel stuck at various points in your life and to struggle to find happiness in your career. You might not realise how normal it is not to know what you want to do and for your career aspirations to change over time. Careers are a work in progress. The dream career might no longer work for you or not in the same way it used to. Often, we think a specific career goal will bring us happiness but either the happiness doesn't last or we don't receive the outcome we had hoped for. The clients' experiences, feelings and emotions below may seem familiar to you, or you may know someone in a similar situation.

Client X had spent relatively short periods of time in multiple jobs. They had never settled, always thinking they needed to move on to find a more suitable role or a different company to work for as things weren't working well. They had recently started a new job and still felt unhappy. They had started to think that they were the problem rather than the job itself and didn't want to repeat the cycle of moving again to a different organisation or into a different role only to feel the same. They needed help to make sense of what was going wrong in their career.

We worked together to explore their values: what truly mattered to them; what motivated them at work; what had been the most meaningful moments at work so far. In a short time, we got clear on what their core needs from work were and the values that were important to them. They were genuinely surprised to discover their underlying values. They had never before consciously thought how this would impact their happiness at work. We could see that their personal values did not align with the company culture, which caused frustration and conflict. This had been an issue in previous roles too. It sounds simple once you know. This led to an understanding of what was behind the unhappiness and a much more informed new job search.

Client Y came to me feeling bored, fed up and at a real career crossroads. They had spent their entire career in the same industry, progressed with promotions and were now at the department head level. It was what they had always aspired to in their career: to be the boss, the senior level leader. It was what they had been working towards, making sacrifices for, on the basis that everything would be great once they had achieved it. Unfortunately, it wasn't great. The reality of the role wasn't what they expected, and they didn't know what to work towards now. The prospect of another twenty years in the same job filled them with dread.

We worked on a structured coaching programme to dig deep into all the necessary elements to find the way forward. We examined their values, strengths, work conditions, and mindset and used all this knowledge to make a career plan for their *what next*. When we finished, Client Y was energised and excited with the new plans, feeling in control of their career happiness and future career direction.

Client Z wasn't entirely sure they needed a coach, but they had been convinced to give it a go by someone who knew it would help. In our initial consultation, they described their job as good and they earned good money. They liked the company they worked for and the people they worked with. It all sounded promising, but I knew a *but* was coming. They said, 'I am wondering *is this it?*' They told me they were not unhappy but wouldn't describe themselves as happy either. We agreed that being able to describe themselves as happy at work was a worthwhile goal. We discussed how this would change not only their professional life but also their personal life. We talked about the impact it would have on people around them.

We worked on how they spent their time, designing their ideal day and week at work. We thought about their vision of career happiness and what career legacy they wanted to leave. After a few sessions, Client Z identified some small changes to practical things concerning how they worked, and a few changes to their mindset regarding how they thought about their career. Even these seemingly small things had a big impact on how they felt. They could now definitely describe themselves as happy with their career.

The recurring themes from people who have received coaching include improved confidence in career choices because they now understand their own priorities, an improved knowledge of their unique abilities, and identification of beliefs they need to let go of. After coaching, clients feel empowered to take control of their future careers, understanding themselves and knowing what will bring happiness.

MY CAREER FULFILMENT DREAM

Imagine a world where everyone does a job they love. No more dreading Monday mornings, no more moaning about work, no more wishing the days away until the weekend or the next holiday. No more thinking *there has got to be more to life!*

Imagine everyone looking forward to going to work, people arriving happy, doing what they are good at, working with people who understand them and what they want and need to be successful. Imagine not just *you* having a job you love, but everyone! What a different world that would be.

My vision for career fulfilment coaching is to make it widely accessible. I want everyone to know what is important to know about themselves when considering their career and how to be happy at work. Career fulfilment should be part of company culture, ensuring they have a happy workforce - and if they don't, changing that. Some organisations invest in coaching for performance enhancement, particular career development points, and for career transitions, but I dream of coaching being available for everyone to support them in pursuit of career happiness. It is not only about people wanting to be paid more, which is what many managers tell me will solve all problems, but managers thinking that shows a problem in itself. It is never just about the money and in lots of cases it is not about money at all! There is so much more than that.

When I discuss career fulfilment coaching with organisations, I sometimes hear resistance from the company to pay for coaching that may result in people leaving the organisation. In some cases this does happen. However, I would be more concerned about someone staying in a job where they weren't happy than investing in coaching and someone leaving. Surely we want people to be happy in the work they do. We know that when workers are happy, they are more productive. We can flip this resistance and see a different perspective: people who have coaching can work through the issues that make them unhappy within their current roles. They can have support to find new perspectives which makes them happier and therefore they decide to stay rather than leave. Coaching for career fulfilment can increase engagement and retention.

I would also love to see a greater focus on people's strengths. People usually enjoy doing what they are good at. I don't know how many hours I have spent in my previous management roles discussing 'weaknesses', things people aren't good at. I agree that we need to look at skill gaps and identify potential blind spots, but this shouldn't be to the detriment of the natural talents of an individual. That could be a whole other chapter, but Martin Seligman, one of the leading figures in positive psychology, said 'build what's strong instead of fix what's wrong' and I fully support this perspective.

Going a step further, all managers and senior leaders should consider coaching an essential skill when the role includes responsibility for individuals within a team. A recent study replaced all managers with coaches with very interesting results, but again that could be a topic for a whole other chapter.

Finally, in my vision for career fulfilment coaching, I want the benefits fully understood and appreciated. I want to support people to embrace the power of coaching to find happiness at work. We can transform the way we approach our careers and ensure every individual finds their career fulfilment.

FINDING YOUR CAREER FULFILMENT

I often encourage clients to think about their career like a book. Are they already at the end of their story enjoying their happily ever after or are they open to a plot twist? Perhaps they are only a few chapters in: they have set the scene and there is so much more to come.

Imagine what the ultimate career story would look like for you. If your career was a published book, what would you like to read? How would you divide your career into chapters?

How important is your career happiness? How happy are you?

If you had to score your career fulfilment on a scale of one to ten, what would you score? If you are not a perfect ten, what could get you closer to a ten? What difference would it make to you, your family, friends and colleagues for you to have an improved score? What impact would that have on your life? Think about the influence on your mental and physical well-being if you woke up wanting to go to work.

What actions can you take now? Small steps can have a significant impact. If you are not in your ideal career and reading this has made you think you would like things to be different, that is already progress. I often tell my clients that their initial consultation call is a pivotal moment. The fact that they have made a conscious decision to do something different, to initiate a change, puts them a massive step closer to where they want to be.

Is there a dream job you have dismissed, never fully explored? Perhaps you believed you weren't good enough; maybe you weren't brave enough or thought it would never work in real life.

I strongly encourage you to consider your work/life priorities. When was the last time you felt excited to go to work? When was the last time you returned home filled with energy from your accomplishments that day? When was the last time you were unhappy with work and thought about the need for change?

While it may not always be easy to find that career where you enjoy your work, you have all the answers within you to have a fulfilling job. Working with a coach will help you unlock those answers. Once you understand what you need to be happy and successful at work and how to achieve it, you can change your life!

> *'Find a job you enjoy doing and you will never have to work a day again in your life.'*
>
> — MARK TWAIN

ABOUT HELEN SCHOEB

Helen Schoeb is a Career Coach and Mentor who helps mid-level managers and senior leaders manage their careers to have fulfilling jobs without sacrificing life outside of work.

Before becoming an accredited coach with the International Coaching Federation (ICF), Helen worked for over twenty years in various senior management roles in financial services. She has also managed her own business. She is an expert on career fulfilment and creating career happiness, and uses her professional knowledge and experience to specialise in helping individuals with career progression and career transitions.

Helen loves live music and regularly attends gigs in London. Originally from the Isle of Man, Helen is drawn to the sea and a sea view is her happy place.

Helen works with clients one-to-one and offers bespoke coaching packages and a career fulfilment coaching programme.

You can contact Helen at:

Email: info@helenschoebcoaching.com
Website: www.helenschoebcoaching.com

linkedin.com/in/helen-schoeb

6

THRIVE USING SAS - SPACE, ACCOUNTABILITY & SUPPORT — JAMES EDER

"PAYING AS YOU VALUE: THE PRICELESS IMPACT OF COACHING"

When I think about coaching, I often think about the Mastercard adverts and the catchphrase, Priceless. Delivered in the right way, I believe coaching can be priceless because of the transformation and the results that can be achieved.

It is easy to spend £50 - £100 out on a meal and drinks and many of us do it without batting an eyelid, and yet, the same people might be reluctant to invest time and money on something life-changing and rewarding such as coaching. Something so transformational that when the work is done, they won't be the same as they were when they started. Instead of thinking about the hourly cost of a coach, if you think about the outcomes that could be achieved or what changes you would like to see and think about what that's worth, this often far exceeds what the cost of the session or package is.

I believe that everyone should have a Coach, not just the Sports players, which is where the foundations of coaching lie, and not just the senior leaders in an organisation. Coaching can help build a strong leadership team and a strong leadership team can make a world of difference.

Take the example of the Clipper Round the World Race, a sailing competition that circumnavigates the globe. All competitors have the same boat, the same food, money, and resources, they all set off at the same time and yet one boat can lead and arrive twenty-four hours earlier than another. It's the individuals on board who come together as a team, the leadership and the roles different people play.

Leadership can be described as taking people on a journey and enabling them to achieve results that alone wouldn't be possible. In the same way, coaching provides an environment for reflection and goal setting around helping individuals or a group of people achieve something that otherwise would not be possible.

My coaching journey began back in 2004 when I was a student at the University of Birmingham. I was passionate about business, and I was always curious about personal development, the performance of people, the power of leadership and what a difference great leadership could make.

As part of their student engagement programme, Cadbury Schweppes invited a group of us to their head offices in Birmingham to receive training that they were going to roll out to the organisation. They wanted to try it on us first – we were their guinea pigs if you like. Whilst I appreciated the opportunity at the time, I had no idea that this would lay the foundation for a career in leadership and making a living out of coaching whilst impacting people in such a profound way.

After I completed my degree, which included a dissertation on the impact coaching has on organisations, I co-founded a business with my brother. Today, that business employs over 250 people.

I started coaching on the back of my second start-up closing. I was diagnosed with a heart condition in 2017 that threw my world into the depths of uncertainty. I knew I wanted to be a coach and support people to achieve success whatever that means to them. In the past, I'd coached and mentored people, but I hadn't charged for it. Now, I knew it was something I not just wanted, but needed to do... So that's what I did. I had honed the foundational coaching principles throughout my career, shaping my leadership style. It was then back in 2021, I trained and qualified as a coach, starting from a place of service and focusing on how I could help people.

THE POWER OF ASKING QUESTIONS VERSUS TELLING SOMEONE WHAT TO DO

As an introduction to coaching, many organisations draw upon the work of former tennis coach, Timothy Gallwey. Instead of instructing, Gallwey discovered that by using a questioning style, successful results would follow. Instead of telling the student to "look at the ball", a line of questioning is used. In his sessions, a volunteer who believes they are weak at catching a ball would be asked to come to the front. A tennis ball would then be repeatedly thrown for them to catch. At the same time as the ball was being thrown, Gallwey would ask questions such as "How is the ball moving towards you?" "How fast is the ball moving?" and "What angle is the ball coming to you at?". The aim of these questions was not to get an accurate answer but to increase focus and awareness of the tennis ball.

As the person improved in catching the ball, Gallwey would ask "How many times in a row do you need to catch the ball for you to say you have been successful?" When a realistic goal, for example, to catch the ball ten times in a row, was suggested and occurred, it could be concluded that coaching had a positive impact.

As focus increases, self-interference decreases, and performance inevitably improves' (Gallwey, 2003, p. 58). The origins of this concept led to the development of the Inner Game series, beginning with the Inner Game of Tennis and followed by the Inner Game of Work.

This was a revolutionary idea to introduce into a field where coaches were often expected to provide answers rather than ask questions.

Clients often come to me looking to find answers to questions. During the exploratory discovery call, I ask clients to describe in their own words what they are looking for. Often, the response is led with descriptors such as clarity, support, and help. The power of coaching comes into its own when clients are given the space to explore what it is they need to do themselves when they have found the solution. They are going to be far more engaged in the outcome if it comes from within instead of being told the solution or what it is that needs to be done by someone externally. It's the same as if someone goes to their manager with a problem. The manager might know the answer but instead of giving it to them, the manager coaches them and asks them the questions that get the employee to come up with the solution. The person leaves empowered and engaged in the outcome, with real ownership instead of feeling micromanaged and disengaged, with a lack of autonomy.

The power of questions is a key element of *The Seven Habits of Highly Effective People* by Stephen Covey. One of the habits is titled 'Start with the End in Mind'. Put simply, it is:

1. Know where you want to go.
2. Know where you are now.
3. What do you need to do to get there?
4. Start, take action.

Success ultimately sits in taking action. By taking action you'll either move closer to where you want to go, in which case, keep doing more, or you'll move further away from where you want to go and if so, stop and do something else.

Often, in the coaching industry, people talk about the importance of having a niche. Who are you serving? What type of person are you trying to help? I've found this conversation with other coaches can often be overwhelming with pressure to find the right focus or not choose the wrong one. I had a different approach. Start with the end in mind.

Had I tried to explain what I am about to share at the beginning of my coaching practice, I would never have been able to. This highlights the power of starting and taking action instead of worrying about the exact focus on positioning who I am as a coach and what am I providing in the first instance. This insight came gradually and was formed over thousands of hours of coaching and helping people achieve success, whatever that means to them, but I was able to refine it into my model:

SAS: WHY DO PEOPLE HAVE A COACH?

I've defined three pillars of why people work with me. These epitomise the fundamentals of coaching. Of course, they aren't limited to just these, but these are the three that seem most important to the clients I've supported over the years.

The first pillar, S, stands for Space.

Often, we are so focused on our day-to-day stresses and challenges that it's hard to see the wood through the trees. Likewise, it's often said that once you've booked the holiday it feels like it's already started. Just knowing you are going can give a sense of relief and excitement. I've found the same is true for my clients (and myself, when I work with my coach). Knowing when the next session is creates the space to reflect and take the time and space that they would otherwise not have taken. Failing that, if they haven't been able to create the space on their own the space can be formed within the session. The time is for them, and the space is created, if for whatever reason they haven't been able to prioritise or create it for themselves.

The second pillar, A, stands for Accountability.

There is huge value and power in not only stating what it is you want to do but sharing it with someone else. It adds another dimension. There's a responsibility to someone else, a feeling of not wanting to let them down. Success ultimately sits in the actions that people take. Inaction is also an action, not making a decision is a decision in itself. At the end of each session, I ask a series of questions; what does the client want to achieve by next time? How committed are they to achieving this? What would it mean to them if it was achieved? Is there anything that would stop them from achieving the outcome? These questions combined can set the client up for success. If, at the next session, they haven't done what they set out to do, it's never for me to reprimand them but ultimately help them understand what's stopped them from achieving the action. Sometimes, naturally, there is the realisation they no longer want to continue the current course of action and it's no longer relevant. Lessons here as to *why* something hasn't been done can be just as valuable as achieving their goal.

The third pillar, S, stands for Support.

Ultimately, I just want to see my clients succeed and my role is to support them to do just that - whatever success means to them. Whilst many of us are fortunate to be surrounded by well-meaning people, everyone has their own motivations. For example, when someone has a business idea and wants to launch something on their own, family and friends may try and talk them out of it. They are likely not meaning to be unkind, but rather they don't want to see the person fail or struggle, so they might not be the best support and may advise against taking the "risk", as they see it.

It's also my role to support and cheer-lead when things are going well just as much as when things aren't going well, and a client needs that ear and voice of encouragement. It's not about what happens or what goes well or goes wrong but how we respond and what we can do to re-frame what's happened.

A powerful question, which might seem uncomfortable at first as it's unfamiliar, is to ask what someone would like to be acknowledged for. Often, we don't get praise or acknowledgement for things we do. It's always interesting to hear people reflect and the answer can be as simple as getting out of bed even though they were struggling and didn't want to. Or investing in themselves and doing the work that is making a big difference for them, which brings me back to my initial point regarding the value of coaching versus the cost.

There are many things coaching can help with - to be happier, and more fulfilled, find a relationship, lose weight, launch a new business, be a better father or mother and of course, the things that can feel more tangible - a promotion or pay rise, for example. If someone got a pay rise of £20,000, would they be willing to pay £2000 for some coaching towards that? No matter what people want, the common theme that comes out is often, people just want to be happier. Often, they may tie their happiness to something external, but that's not necessarily the answer. For example, they may think "If I get a new job/new house/new car/new relationship, then I'll be happy." But it can be tiring, the constant chasing and need for new things. I've found this can be part of the coaching process - the realisation that takes place for the client over time as shorter-term goals are realised and the bigger questions are then asked: What do they really want on a deeper level? Are they fulfilled? What is their purpose? What experiences do they want? How do they want to contribute to society? These are all elements that are important to explore and can contribute to the overall outcome of being truly happy.

My coaching experience has been most successful when I paid for sessions as there was a value exchange. With payment came expectations, not simply of the person delivering the sessions for me but also of myself. It forced me to take the time to prepare and also follow up on sessions, otherwise, what was the point in me paying for it? Whilst I felt the same when it was free, there must be an exchange that way both people feel they are getting value more than simply the idea of helping and feeling good about it. There are lots of organisations or people who are willing to help like this and provide these types of sessions for free and if that's for you, I encourage you to seek those out.

The most common approach to coaching you'll see is where coaches charge per session or for a block of sessions as part of a programme or series - either 121 or in a group setting. To flip this on its head I was keen to create something accessible and engage clients with the question upfront as to how they value the work they do with me, linking directly to their goal and what they want to achieve. Shortly before I started with my first clients, I was in Westfield Shopping Centre and saw a pay-as-you-massage service where, at the end, you pay what you feel it was worth. It seemed to me that this approach could work for coaching and mentoring, and this is what I came up with - a pay-what-you-value approach. I am charging for my time, with the ethos of charging fairly whilst making sure it is affordable and accessible. It has been an amazing experience which really acts as a way to help clients focus on the future and outcomes whilst putting value on the work they are doing with me.

Whilst it's easy to think by default they are buying an hour of your time - a significant amount of work gets done by the client in between sessions. A transformational coaching experience on reflection can really mean one plus one does equal three. The sum impact of the coaching over time is greater than the per-hour sessions which can be seen as very transactional. The most successful clients I've seen are the ones who enter the partnership with the clarity of what they want to achieve within a set time frame. As milestones are achieved it's easier to re-contract and build out the next series of sessions on the back of success instead of a client buying a six-month or twelve-month programme up front.

Over the years, I've worked with clients who have used my services as a coach giving them the Space, Accountability and Support they've needed to succeed. Understanding my approach, I thought the best way to bring what I do to life is to share a couple of examples of what coaching has done for a couple of my clients, shared anonymously, of course, with their permission.

Firstly, a seasoned marketing professional who helped launch brands and built his career as the world digitised. He embraced new technologies and was at the forefront of the new way of working online. He reached out to me on the back of an email I shared about my life updates and that I was now offering coaching. Initially, it was a general catch-up call, but it turned into a call where he shared that he was at a crossroads, keen to start his own business but not sure where to start and how to get his first clients.

We took some time to explore some of the limiting beliefs that were holding him back as well as the assumptions that were being made of what was needed and how things needed to be. Starting with the end in mind, he came up with the figure that £10,000 in revenue a month would be a healthy target and something he wanted to aspire to.

The coaching initially focused on questions such as how many clients were needed to deliver on the £10,000 who and what the ideal client would look like, what sectors the clients were in, where would he find the clients and the low-hanging fruits, as well as identifying the opportunity of sharing what he was now doing with his existing network and previous employers and allowing them to work with him.

For the first few months, we worked through concerns around positioning and ultimately, instead of refining the offering he understood the opportunity of a more consultative approach, asking potential clients what they needed and tailoring responses. He found he spent a lot of work and time on proposals to understand what the client needed and then not getting the work so instead, we reflected on a better way - to charge clients for the initial piece of work which gets their buy-in. It was also identified that there was some fear of rejection in sharing what they were doing and not being comfortable with selling. I coached him around re-framing this as an opportunity and provided clarity, reframing his beliefs around how he is there to provide support and help to people and make a real difference for their businesses. He proceeded to hit the £10,000-a-month target after gaining the four to five clients he needed.

Over the last two years, as we've had our monthly sessions, whilst there have been challenges, there has also been a real transformation. The client is not the same person who started with me. He's grown in confidence immeasurably and now he consistently gets the business he tenders for. He also decided to bring his health goals into our sessions. He started going to the gym again and made a conscious decision to stop drinking alcohol.

Using the three pillars and creating space each month for me and our sessions, along with the consistent action-taking in between sessions, is truly inspiring. It's incredible to be on the sidelines to watch and know I've been part of this transformation. He's done the heavy lifting. I'm just grateful he's trusted me to go on this journey with him. Each session, he reflects on what's been done, and what hasn't and the accountability that it provides is often referenced. During the month, even though we are not together he checks in by email or messages to let me know how the gym workout is going or that it's been over a year since he's had any alcohol. As we're in touch in between sessions, I am supporting him and cheerleading his successes. I help him to understand that it's okay when things aren't on track and that he has the opportunity to get back on track again each and every day - which he does, time and time again.

My second example of a client is someone who had run a start-up with some co-founders after raising the initial investment. Unfortunately, the business didn't work out. At the time he reached out to me, he was working for a company in a full-time position, but he knew he wanted to go again, and he knew he wanted some support from a coach to help him get there. This time it was going to be different, and he wanted to give himself every chance of success.

I remember our initial discovery call, over four years ago. He knew about me through the start-up community. Whilst being a coach doesn't mean you need to be an expert on the subject matter in the field you work in, I positioned myself as someone who focuses on working with people in the start-up space. I've experienced both success and failure with my own start-ups and often, the lessons from failure can be far greater than success. With 9/10 businesses failing within the first three years, knowing when to give up or when to continue can be a big consideration and challenge for many entrepreneurs. Founders can also have an incredibly lonely journey and even when co-founding with someone, the loneliness can still pervade.

The approach in this case was simple. He had a business idea he wanted to work through and validate and he wanted to start the process of leaving his current job to launch his own business. He wanted to commit to ten sessions. At the end of the ten sessions, we would review and see if there was an opportunity to continue. That was over four years ago, and we've had weekly sessions since.

Often, despite all good intentions, the day job and living life can be all-consuming and just too much to be able to start thinking about starting something new. That said, each week my client reflected on what he wanted to do, setting up actions to be done with accountability for the following week and receiving the validation and encouragement to keep moving forward.

A pivotal session came when he shared that he wanted to go down to four days a week and he was going to do it in four weeks. I asked what was stopping him from doing it sooner. What would the impact be if he was able to do it sooner? The barrier was the fear of having that conversation with his current employer. A shift came in the realisation that going down to four days a week was really important and would make a big difference in starting the new venture. Even though there was concern in asking the question, the sooner the request was in, the sooner it would happen. The conversation and request to go down to four days a week happened a month ahead of the original plan and it was agreed that he could start at the beginning of the next month.

All too often, it's the fear of the unknown that stops us in our tracks- the worry about how someone else might respond. This results in us not living our best lives and compromising on what we really want. As you read this, think about something that you might be putting off - a decision that you want to make or a change you know will make a big difference for you. Perhaps it's on your mind but you keep dismissing it, telling yourself it's not a problem. Imagine if that change had already taken place, what would that mean to you? How do you think you would feel? As you consider this and take action to do something about it (which could even be as simple as having that conversation you've been putting off), remember that it's in these moments that things change, the transformation happens and you are living in a different world, a new reality where something else is now possible.

Week by week, my client gradually worked less and less for his existing employer. He registered his new business, the domain name, the first employees, a freelance designer, and the sales deck and finally left to go full-time. Then came the first clients, the first revenue and the growth, more clients, client success, validation, product-market fit, partnerships revenue growth, challenges with employees, work-life balance, aspirations to take time to travel… Over four years in the business of doing business, we've been on a journey. He's consistently shown up and this year, is on track to do £1m turnover.

In the turmoil that followed the diagnosis of my heart condition, coaching came to me in what feels like a gift, providing me with the ability to help people and the flexibility to live and travel adjusting to the different seasons and times of the year. All my clients are aware of my challenges, which are set out as part of my onboarding process and discovery calls as it's important to me for clients to understand that my motivation is all geared towards helping them, providing the space, accountability, and support for them to succeed, whatever success means to them.

My aim for any call, including the free discovery call, is to make a difference, however small, for my clients. To leave them better than I found them, or when they found me. There were times in the last few years when my heart health deteriorated but despite being bed-bound on some days, I would get up, have a shower, get dressed and show up for my clients, no matter how hard it was. At the time they didn't necessarily know it, but it felt so rewarding to know that I was valued and there for them even in some of my most difficult times. I'm so grateful to them for trusting me, sharing with me, and allowing me to help support them on their journeys.

ABOUT JAMES EDER

James Eder is an entrepreneur and Work.Life coach. He has over twenty years of experience in various leadership roles. In 2005, he graduated from the University of Birmingham, having completed his dissertation on the impact of coaching in Organisations. Since then, he has been on a continuous self-development journey, sharing his experience and knowledge as a mentor and coaching people, helping support their adventures. In 2021, James completed an ACC ICF-accredited programme with Optimus Academy.

He is the Co-Founder of StudentBeans, a company that set out to empower students to thrive. The student discount platform quickly became a global leader providing brands with student verification, gen z insights and advertising services. StudentBeans continues as part of a new company identity, Pion, which brings together an ecosystem of products and services; Insights, Advertising & Verification.

Following the discovery of his heart condition, Hypertrophic Cardiomyopathy, he has designed a life to work for him. Recently, James has focused on leveraging his experience and expertise as a Work.Life coach, delivering transformation for his clients. Focusing on entrepreneurs, founders and people who know they want to make changes in their lives, he gives them SAS - Space, Accountability and Support - to help them be the best they already are.

He can be reached here:

Web: www.jameseder.com
Telephone: 00 44 7734 866 968

linkedin.com/in/jameseder

7

COACHING WHEN YOU ARE 'NEUROSPICY' — KASEY PETROWSKI

EMBRACING AUTHENTICITY AND NEURODIVERSITY, AND CANCELING TOXIC POSITIVITY

MOMENTS OF IMPACT

Would you join me in a quick visualization? Go to your favorite playlist. Put on **that** song. That one that you feel in your chest. That song that causes you to close your eyes and put your hand to your heart and feel that tingling sensation rush through your body. Maybe it makes you get up and dance. Maybe it causes you to recall a memory or a feeling in your life. Perhaps that memory isn't a memory yet and you feel anticipation for when it is.

Once you have that song, I invite you to relax your shoulders, relax your jaw, take a deep breath, close your eyes, and visualize the last impactful moment that happened in your life. See you now, looking at you then. Watch the moment of impact that ultimately changed the way you thought your next chapter would be - everything you were feeling, every emotion that came up for you in that moment. Take a moment.

As you bring that awareness forward, how did that moment of impact lead you to the life you are experiencing right now, in this version of you? What has it taught you about yourself?

Much like this book, you will experience different chapters, different seasons, and different moments of impact in your coaching journey. It will take you down roads you didn't know you were able to travel and create new versions of yourself, allowing you to be the believer and advocate in someone else's life story as well as your own. There will be individuals, clients, and 'coachees' whose lives will change because of you… and your life will change as a result.

Our moments of impact drive us to make decisions, reconnect with ourselves and others, and finally seek that support we have been needing to make life decisions, big or small. Those moments of impact contribute to chapters in our life stories. Human experiences drive us to think, feel, behave, and do. While I know this 'feels' like one hundred pounds of weight on each shoulder, and you are trying to stand tall with confidence and be the 'resilient Coach' through it all - know that this journey that we choose, for most of us, won't be what we initially think it is.

I have had the greatest of opportunities, being able to play a role as an Accredited Coach who is also *Neurodivergent** (see chapter glossary for this term). My diagnoses say I have deficits in:

"…social-emotional reciprocity, ranging, for example, from abnormal social approach and failure of normal back-and-forth conversation; to reduced sharing of interests, emotions, or affect; to failure to initiate or respond to social interactions."

"difficulties in sustaining relationships and in feeling close to others."

These statements appear isolating and indefinite, don't they?

How can I coach someone to their greatest potential if I am defined by an 1800s textbook and misunderstood because of societal stigmas?

But that textbook and those stigmas fail to see my unconditional devotion to the emotions that I experience with others. They cannot feel the intensity of the emotions that I absorb for and with others: feelings of elation and happiness for my clients, to moments of "I don't think I've got this", to feeling defeated for my clients when they've experienced the unimaginable, to channeling the confidence that emulates a character I aspire to, Wendy Rhoades, Performance Coach from the show *Billions*.

I wondered if my Autism Spectrum Disorder (ASD) and Complex Post Traumatic Stress Disorder (C-PTSD) would ultimately sabotage my passion for Coaching, and whether I would do myself a disservice by telling clients I am Autistic?

This led me to question my purpose and identity, the very thing I was to coach others through.

This experience felt a lot like bungee jumping, but through it I've also had the greatest of opportunities to watch all the individuals I work with add a new painting to their life mural, add that next scene to their life movie, add a new soundtrack to their life album, add another chapter to their life story.

Let's explore this adventure, together.

OPEN YOURSELF TO EXPERIENCING ALL THE PARTS, NOT JUST THE 'GOOD ONES'

Becoming a Coach was not always my dream role. In fact, I didn't know what to call it for many years. I assumed a 'Coach' led a sports team. I could only ever describe 'coaching' as a physical and outward sensation that I experience. When I can help others fall in love with their life story is much like when I've found a new song that I '*stim** on' (see chapter glossary) and cannot stop playing.

My eyes light up, sparkling with eagerness and anticipation. I wear a genuine, heartwarming smile that's like that rare ray of sunshine peeking in during the winter season of the Northeast of the United States. There's a warm, glowing energy that starts in my chest and radiates outward, like the roots of a tree expanding and creating a foundation that is truly alive.

In the voices of the people I experience, I hear the symphony of transitioning in their voices. I hear that first "Wow" as they have their first insight into something they've never visualized before. Their ideas and connection to purpose become more melodious, and the expressions of gratitude are like the sweetest notes of your favorite song, filling the air with harmony.

Having the opportunity to indulge in this *special interest** (see chapter glossary) is a bit like the sweet satisfaction of your favorite dessert, that feeling when you savor each bite of impact, shift, and transformation. It's a taste of the joy that comes from guiding someone to rediscover the deliciousness of their own existence.

Their air seems fresher - and you as the Coach carry the scent of new beginnings. It is like a bouquet of your favorite smells intertwined together creating nostalgia as though you've been here before, and maybe you have. It is a reminder that every person's life story is unique and can be fallen in love with again and again like the first time you met your favorite person, that first time you watched your favorite movie.

These sensations are what I feel in my prime of being a professional thought partner to someone. But I want to be clear here - this journey is not always uplifting; it's not coaching to a step-by-step process or a 'fail-proof' one. You must open yourself to experiencing every part of this journey, not just the 'good sessions'.

I hadn't opened myself up to this notion when I began. I'd say any positive mantra to myself, trying to visualize how I could make my clients feel on top of the world before our session even began, trying to be that perfectly resilient coach with the most thought-provoking questions. Only this went against our core competency #5 "Maintains Presence".

I learned this with my first client, Rebecca (she/her). This is a short story written with a Disney flair (because, why not?). Actual names, roles, and company redacted for privacy.

Cue Part of Your World by Ariel

Once upon a time in a bustling enchanting city there lived hard-working business wizards whose mission was to help top wizardry organizations see their process efficiencies through to success with just a tap of their magical wands (and master analytical skills). In their magical corporate fortress was Rebecca, a Certified Business Wizard. She worked for the prestigious 'MagiTech Enterprises', a company known for captivating high-end products and innovative wizardry. Rebecca had always been passionate about the work she accomplished and was well-versed in her craft. She was even voted 'Top Business Wizard' on her team.

While she had many other magical business consultants around her, something wasn't quite right. Heavy sensations of disconnection and, "Why does everyone seem like they know what's going on and I don't?" wrapped their invisible tendrils around her mind, slowly eroding her self-confidence. Each morning, as she entered the corporate fortress, Rebecca couldn't shake the sensation of feeling like an imposter at the company. She watched her colleagues work together seamlessly, joking, and collaborating on projects with just a flick of their wands, and she felt like an outsider. She wanted this connection, collaboration and unity, too.

Rebecca knew she needed support, but wasn't sure where to turn and who she could turn to safely. There was no Workplace Fairy Godmother who could instantly tap the imposter syndrome and discomfort away. Feeling nearly defeated, she'd sigh and reluctantly open her LinkedIn. Her newsfeed refreshed to a post created by me. A post about coming out as a Neurodivergent Coach in Training. Curious and recalling a past Coaching experience she'd had before, she reached out to ask if I had space for her. I was very new to Ruth's program, and therefore, new to Coaching.

The concepts she brought to our first session were:

- **Imposter** syndrome
- **Diminished** self-confidence
- **Limited space** for career growth
- **Outcasted** community

I tried to process where I could help her start. I swallowed hard in my throat, nervous sweating. The thoughts began to flood in.

"I don't know what to say."

"But I am still learning."

"What if I mess this up and I can't help her see the magic that is within her?"

"She doesn't know I'm Autistic."

"What if it shows?"

"Kasey, say something!"

Imposter Syndrome? Me too. I stood there on Zoom, frozen. I wanted to hide behind my own self, was crippled by my thoughts, and was immediately discrediting myself before we even got to the first, "Where would you like to begin today's session?" Just like I was taught.

Trust and be trusted. I took a deep breath. I knew I couldn't begin this journey hiding behind myself anymore.

"Rebecca, thank you for being vulnerable with me. It's now time for me to be vulnerable with you as your Coach should you choose to work with me."

"I'm Autistic and have a diagnosis of Complex Post Traumatic Stress Disorder. This means I have a different perception of the world around me, and there are times I need a little help, too, for us to be successful."

"There may be times when I might need to have you repeat things because my brain didn't process them fast enough."

"I also too fast think (think too fast)...

and need to pause...

before I speak so I do not my sentences jumble."

"I take notes to help me recall what we've discussed throughout the session, otherwise, my brain tends to become flooded. Like a boiling pot of water, it spills over and is gone from my memory. I am always happy to send you the notes after our sessions."

"I am in training for professional coaching, I'm still learning a lot and I won't get this 'right' every time, but my special interest is helping people see the next chapter in the life they want to create for their life story. Does working with someone who is neurodivergent give you anxiety? I can understand if you don't want..."

To which she inserted, "Absolutely not. In fact, I am more excited to work with you knowing this."

Hiding my anxiety and preparation for rejection, I unclenched my jaw, relaxed my shoulders, and logged that interaction as a moment of impact for me. When I trusted her that I could share a vulnerability about myself within a few minutes of meeting her, she trusted me with some of the deepest parts of her life she wished to share.

I took one more breath. "Okay you've mentioned quite a few things here," I said. I repeated them back to her:

"Imposter syndrome.
Diminished self-confidence.
Limited space for career growth.
Outcasted community."

"On a scale of severity and thinking about what is causing the most stress for you right now, which one of those would you like to begin unpacking in today's session?"

Rebecca and I worked together for over a year. She was the person who kickstarted my journey into Coaching and was there to celebrate me when I received my accreditation (with all the imperfections and *neurospicy** (see chapter glossary) in between). There are not enough words that can be listed in this chapter for how grateful I was to not only have the space, but to advocate for that space to be created to be vulnerable, show imperfection, and to show that not every session was meant to be a 'life transformation session'. That's not how growth happens.

Growth happens when we are least ready for it, least wanting it, and least expecting it. When I focused on being Rebecca's thought partner and not a 'life transformation performance coach', I was able to provide her with that genuine, protective, and intimate space so she could come to the understanding that what she actually sought was **comfort** within her work environment and role, not a higher self-confidence, as well as **connection** to others in the workplace. We would continue down this path to help her understand her communication preferences, team cohesiveness, and ways of working as well as how these preferences and ways of working differ from those of her colleagues.

Here's what Rebecca had to say about the experience with me (permission has been granted to share):

"[I entered Coaching to] improve my confidence and gain clarity on roles/areas of interest within [The Company]. It made me focus on myself and what I want to improve. It helped me think of things from a different perspective. There were numerous 'aha' moments that overall will just make me a better learner, communicator, and teammate. Mostly I focused on work-related items, but the coaching did lead me to discuss some things with my closest family members. I wasn't sure what to expect but found this focus time during coaching led me to other resources and discussions that were really beneficial. Thank you so much for all of the coaching through my projects and helping me build my confidence. It's still a work in progress but I am so grateful [The Company] allowed you to work with some of us. I have found it invaluable and don't think I would have made it through the last year without your support." – Rebecca

A truly magical experience and moment of impact for both of our life chapters.

Remember, you may not be changing someone's life every session; and as Coaches, we need to learn how to be comfortable coming to terms with this. Since Rebecca, I've made it a vow to myself to allow the hard sessions, allow the imperfect. The sessions that didn't go quite right. The sessions that left me questioning if I was really cut out for this.

When a musician creates an album, they don't focus on creating songs that only emulate feelings of 'joy', 'motivation', and 'growth'; or those that only emulate feelings of 'curiosity', 'anxiety', or 'defeat'. Combining those emotions together, the artist can connect their listeners to a universal human experience. We all understand that life is complex; not one person's life story is 'simply told'.

I don't believe in spewing out toxic positivity in every negative experience our clients have. When things are hard, instead of constantly reframing our negative thoughts like they shouldn't exist, gaslighting ourselves or others, let them be hard. There's not always going to be a positive reframe for every single negative outcome and it isn't beneficial for us as Coaches to make our clients believe this. Sure, there is something to be said about helping someone see the light coming from the lighthouse up ahead, but when there are rough waters we need to acknowledge this and ensure that we model a, "I'll ride these rough waters with you until we get to that lighthouse - where that extraordinary entrance is."

It doesn't help my client who has lost their significant other to a vicious and unforgiving battle of cancer to say, "Let's try and think of this from a positive angle; what's something positive that came from this?"

Be willing and human enough to sit with your clients in the complexities, bungee jumping from motivation to demotivation, to growth, then to setback, from learning, to stagnation for the moment. It is never our call to say when each chapter of their reality should be over, when their song on that soundtrack should end, or when they should stop painting that mural. Those complexities in their reality, their voice, their body language... *that* is their reality at that moment, not what you want their reality to be. When things are hard, let them be hard for the moment.

My client survey measured their overall experience (what they hoped to get out of coaching versus what they received), the feasibility of coaching (did it 'fit' as they imagined it would into the rest of their life?), and which tools helped them the most/least. The results showed a ninety-five percent satisfaction rate with specific notes on my presence with them, a one hundred percent feasibility rate, and a zero percent report that my Neurodivergence prevented them from succeeding in their goals and their next challenge in their lite story.

"Kasey is an empathetic listener and observer. She has a way to let you open up yourself and share personal stories. Besides discussing work-relevant topics, we also chatted a lot on personal life."

"I feel different than I did when I started the coaching sessions. Forcing myself to see myself from other perspectives has been key. I've always been very good at looking at the other person's viewpoint or side of things. It's much harder to see yourself the way others do. I thrive in an environment where I add value and these sessions have helped me see that I am thriving and focus on those wins (big and small)."

"My conversations with Kasey have been helpful not just for my professional life but for my personal life as well. I feel comfortable sharing certain challenges that I may be facing outside of work, especially mental and emotional challenges, and many times, just talking through these feelings can help me relieve some internal frustration. I have also set some personal goals, such as getting my driver's permit and license and going on a solo trip, that I got a lot of encouragement from Kasey about that I really appreciate."

They don't need you to be the perfect Coach, they need a present one. Sessions in which I was truly present with a client allowed me to help myself as a Coach and I introduced my clients to Coaching as it really is. It is not telling them what we think they should do; it is not giving them our solutions to their challenges.

Your clients trust you to allow that space of rough open waters *before* they reach their extraordinary entrance to the lighthouse. When you trust, you can be trusted. Remember, their growth is not your responsibility, but you should be in their corner. Coach in a way that serves them to find *their* inner guru, not yours.

GIVE YOURSELF THE GIFT YOU GIVE TO OTHERS

Through Coaching others, I was able to improve many things in my own life, but ultimately, I watched as my presence transformed from hanging on to every last word in a lyrical ballad to just listening and feeling, and trusting that the rest will come as it needs to. There can be so much unnecessary pressure in Coaching, especially when you're 'Neurospicy AF'. There have been coaching sessions where I've simply asked, "What if we didn't call this a 'Coaching Session' today?" and, "What if we didn't 'Coach' today?" so that the conversation would eliminate pressure to perform (on both sides) and focus on being a thought partner on whatever came up holistically.

In the world of Coaching, there's so much discussion on who we help, but not who has helped *us*. My clients have helped me in ways that I've shared with them. I don't believe 'shared successes' go one way. Sure, we have competencies, ethics, and morals that we follow as Accredited Coaches, but at the end of the day, we are all still humans who need connection.

I used to rehearse every single conversation, being Autistic, and my clients have helped me realize I don't need to do that. They don't care that I am Autistic, they care that I am in their corner. I can breathe again without having to rehearse 'as much'. I say 'as much' because I still rehearse and practice conversations in certain situations. I'll never put the pressure on myself to stop rehearsing. It's helped me often, but it was a change in direction that without Coaching, I perhaps would have never experienced.

Whereas I used to cling to big buzzwords in the Organizational Behavior, Industrial-Organizational Psychology, and Coaching spaces (and sometimes I still do, they are my special interests after all) I now allow human interactions to be as raw, complex, and imperfect as they actually are. Clients often tell me they gravitated toward me because of my 'calm' presence, and my 'genuine' and 'fair' outlook on life's possibilities and challenges. I don't promise to reframe every negative thought to a positive one in every scenario.

If the idea of 'perfectionism' or "I need to be positive every second of my day!" is projected onto the Coach and/or is projected in the coaching environment during any session, I challenge the Coach to see that as an opportunity to coach themselves and/or the client through why that could be happening:

"Is there anyone in your life who makes you feel like you need to be perfect?"
"Who in your life story needs you to be perfect?"
"What would it be like to let this session be imperfect?"
"What could be accomplished if we allow our imperfect to shine through today?"

Invited to the Neurospicy party with Autism, and where the crippling C-PTSD resulted, I had quite a traumatic childhood which, has led me to the greatest lessons on humility, the gift of being a giver and the power in the pause.

In addition to a series of awesome therapists, my husband and daughter were part of my life's greatest moments of impact and transformation. They helped me see that I was the one forcing perfectionism in nearly every area of my life. It wasn't until I could ask myself those above questions that CEO of her own life, Kasey Petrowski, could start calling the other board members to take control: 'Rapunzel' to take control of creativity, 'Merida' to take control of courage, 'Wendy Rhoades' to take control of confidence.

Through coaching myself, I was able to give myself my own voice back – much like Ariel in *The Little Mermaid*. Through my ability to coach others, I was able to help mothers see possibilities beyond motherhood, a military spouse to find meaning in a life beyond serving their spouse's career, business consultants realize their 'why' and understand their relationship with their customers as a partnership. I've watched leaders realize when they have been lacking self-awareness or have not fostered an environment of trust with their direct reports, individual contributors finally receive that promotion to a manager role, and a member of the armed forces have a new insight that they can start a new life beyond service to their country.

I KNOW IT IS A CLICHÉ, BUT BE THE CHANGE YOU WANT TO SEE

I want to see a larger transformation in the Coaching industry. I have seen amazing Accredited Coaches, but I've also seen amazing Coaches who were not accredited, and they were just as successful as their accredited counterparts. With any industry that is not regulated, you are bound to see a lot of 'grays'. I don't dislike the 'gray'. I think we need 'gray' to not function like robots in our sessions; however, I do believe in energies. As a 'deep feeler', I know when someone is truly in my corner, and when they are giving me fluff for their 'Six Figure Coaching Business' and they haven't asked about my story.

I want to see a Coaching industry that considers the simplicity in being a 'thought partner' but doesn't get so comfortable in simplicity that we overlook growth. I want to see a Coaching industry that doesn't glorify forced positivity but knows when to provide another insight into life that hasn't yet been explored. I want to see a Coaching industry that can blend a mix of consulting or therapy if that Coach has the credentials to do so, but to know that they can only take their client as far as they've gone themselves. The 'gray' can open so many possibilities and allows for genuine growth. As Accredited Coaches, how can we do this in the most ethical way possible? As both Coach and Coachee, you must be protective over your time (their time) and your space (their space). Get rid of the 'culture killers', 'energy vampires' or however you identify them. You may ask yourself and your clients:

"Who (or what) adds to my / your energy?"
"Who (or what) depletes my / your energy?"

Be protective of your time and who you allow in that space. Being clear about that is being kind.

Naturally, being Autistic, I love a routine and a process to follow. It is not in my nature to navigate to something that is out of routine or out of process. This does not allow for much of a 'gray' area. Different social interactions through my coaching sessions have allowed me to open my mind to see that no one coaching practice is ever the 'go-to'. I won't always use G.R.O.W, I won't always need Somatic Coaching, and I do not always need Transactional Analysis. That's okay.

When I focus on being their thought partner, I can choose from a 'coaching wardrobe' when something might be a good fit; on the contrary, when a coaching approach is not working, I am not afraid to switch the soundtrack to the next song. You must have the humility to admit to yourself when you need to abandon an approach. It is not about what you've been able to do for Client A that is now not working for Client B. Stay present, allow your clients to guide you on their winding path, and offer new paths (new ways of thinking, feeling, being) when they are ready.

OUR PERCEIVED STRUGGLES CAN BE OUR GREATEST SUPERPOWERS

Not one client shared - in person, or through survey - that my disabilities were a distraction or otherwise 'got in the way' of their success in our Coaching sessions. My projections onto myself were a distraction and 'got in the way' until I stopped making it about me. It was never about me in the first place.

Coaching we serve, but we also have a very deep-rooted understanding that humans are 'complex' because life is complex. We must strive to build resiliency in our lives, but give ourselves the grace that others give us. Being Neurodivergent or having a mental illness does not prevent anyone from being a great thought partner. Our greatest struggle or challenge can be our greatest serving superpower for others.

To date, I don't have the answer for being a great coach. This chapter wasn't made for that. I don't know if my ideology or approach is 'correct' or 'incorrect'; there will be changes to our industry in the foreseeable future that we aren't in control of.

What we are in control of is the experience and presence people receive when they sit with us, when they listen to a new soundtrack to their life album that wasn't there before, when they flip to a new chapter of their life story they weren't expecting, when that 'dream scene' in their life movie just became their reality. You helped them speak it into existence, visualize it, write it down - maybe in a list or in the form of a future letter to their future selves. That's what it is like to be a thought partner.

When I get closer to the end of my life story, the 'perfect coaching approach' or 'the perfect coach' will turn out not to be as important as we thought. What will matter to me when I am at the end of my life story is that I won't have to wonder,

"What would it have been like to be a Coach?"

GLOSSARY OF TERMS

Neurodivergent - "a non-medical umbrella term that describes people with variation in their mental functions, and can include conditions such as autism spectrum disorder (ASD) or other neurological or developmental conditions such as attention-deficit/hyperactivity disorder (ADHD)" (Courtney & Gregory, Forbes, 2023).

Stimming ("stim") - "The term "stimming," short for self-stimulating behaviors, refers to repetitive or ritualistic movements or sounds that help an individual self-soothe when stressed or otherwise cope with their emotions" (*Psychology Today*, 2023).

Special Interest - "When viewed as strengths and opportunities, special interests become pathways to helping adults with autism experience happiness and well-being, live, find meaning and purpose, and build relationships and communities–worthy goals for neurodivergent *and* neurotypical people alike" (*Psychology Today*, 2023).

Neurospicy - A fun term used when one describes and relates their personal experience of being Neurodivergent to that of spicy food. It can describe the intensity of what it is like to be Neurodivergent, and courage to embrace a differing brain and non-traditional human experience from that of a 'typical' human brain and traditional human experience (Petrowski [Personal Opinion], 2023).

ABOUT KASEY PETROWSKI

Kasey Petrowski, a dedicated thought partner for individuals who seek to uncover their extraordinary life stories, draws inspiration from a life of raw and diverse experiences. As a Neurodivergent mother and dedicated military spouse, she has had to navigate the challenges of constant change with resilience and grace. Kasey is a passionate advocate for mental health, bringing awareness, openness, and understanding to the intersection of being a Neurodivergent individual with both Autism (ASD) and Complex Post Traumatic Stress Disorder (C-PTSD).

Playing in her current role (character) as a Business Analyst and Process Improvement Specialist, Kasey champions her skill as a continuous improvement wizard, applying analytical skills to enhance efficiency and effectiveness in various aspects of life. Doubling as an ICF-accredited Coach, Kasey effortlessly channels her natural talent to guide others, encouraging them to maintain a sense of curiosity throughout their journey of self-discovery.

Her refuge lies in the realm of words, where she artfully shares experiences related to neurodivergence and the haunting, yet enlightening impact of childhood trauma. Through her writing, Kasey invites curious minds into a world where vulnerability becomes a captivating source of empowerment and understanding. Illuminating the path toward healing, she fosters a community where diverse voices are embraced and each life story holds an unknown that is worth discovering.

Contact:

linkedin.com/in/kasey-petrowski

8

THE TRUE BEAUTY OF COACHING — MARY PHILLIPS

One of the things I love most about coaching is that you never know how a session will turn out. For instance, a session may start with a client expressing a seemingly straightforward goal, such as improving time management. However, as we delve deeper, it could unfold into a realisation that underlying self-doubt is a significant obstacle.

The true beauty of coaching lies in its capacity to navigate uncharted territories of the mind—a client might seek career advice only to reveal an unexplored passion that leads to a potential career change. Sessions can unexpectedly transform into a powerful exploration of limiting beliefs, personal values, or hidden aspirations. What might appear as a routine topic can be a profound self-discovery journey, unravelling layers of thought patterns and unveiling untapped potential.

I am deeply grateful to have been exposed to coaching early in my life. I experienced a lightbulb moment around clarity and my purpose: serving. This exposure, combined with my background in healthcare, has allowed my coaching approach to develop in an inherently holistic way. It seeks to comprehensively address the interconnected challenges of life, recognising the importance of addressing issues not in isolation but as part of an extensive, interconnected system. This holistic approach allows for a profound and transformative exploration, fostering a deeper understanding of the complexities that shape an individual's experiences and well-being.

As a teenager, I worked Saturdays at Stroud public library (Gloucestershire, UK). My role was mainly to reshelve returned books and to check books in and out. Shelving was repetitive and heavy work. The full-timers saved the overloaded trolleys for me. I wouldn't say I liked it to begin with, but at some point, I realised I had a choice: I could either grumble like the rest of the team, or I could find the silver lining. I decided to time myself shelving - see how many books I could shelve in the shortest amount of time. Once my trolleys were empty, I would systematically work around the library, ensuring the books were correctly shelved in order, using the Dewey Decimal Classification method.

The non-fiction books were organised around the edges of the library, with the fiction in the middle. This meant there were nooks where I could loiter with little interruption as I began to explore the covers of the books, mainly the more colourful non-fiction. I found the personal development books particularly enthralling; I spent my breaks with my nose in whichever book sparked my senses that shift. One of the first books I read was on speed reading - which was probably more luck than judgment, but it has saved me a lot of time over the years. With my new reading talent, I devoured them. Nothing beats the smell and texture of fresh paper and the feeling of flicking through the pages of a crisp new book. There was a promise of a different life through the knowledge gleaned from advice. I would stay awake reading when I should have been revising for my A levels. These books reassured me that if I implemented their strategies, I would have the power to create a better destiny than I ever dreamed possible. But only if I did the work. If only osmosis worked with knowledge, too.

This love of paper also extended to most stationery, which I used to compile a list of goals. When I graduated at twenty-five years of age, a good friend invited me to join her at a United Chiropractic Association (UCA) conference. The aim of the UCA association is to help their members lead and maintain a healthier lifestyle, and to offer drug-free spinal health care and advice. I entered a room of hundreds of people with a similar mindset; the atmosphere was electric, full of happy people looking for ways to improve themselves and their clients. I found myself at home in that room. The optimist in me lapped up what was said and jotted the nuggets of wisdom down in an A5-sized notebook. I hadn't been to an event like it before. I was a member of a more reserved association and this conference was a pivotal turning point when I started to look at health from an alternative perspective. From the inside out. Something that we create.

At each event since, live or online, I have continued to record things that spark me, and I have loads of these notebooks brimming with inspiration. From time to time, when flicking through them, something will catch my attention; contained in it is a message – usually something reminding me that I have the power inside me to achieve anything and everything I want, from walking on fire to jumping out of a helicopter (with a parachute!).

After one of these events, I bought a self-directed course from an Australian Chiropractor and Coach. Her course created several lightbulb moments for me, specifically around community building. I implemented everything, and this was the foundation of building an incredibly successful clinic from scratch, which is still thriving twenty years on. I set a series of goals to achieve: business goals and financial goals. Within five years, I had paid off my £60k student debt; my husband and I had bought a house and paid off the mortgage. I had my own successful business with a great team around me. In my thirtieth year, I became a mummy, which was the top of my list, something I will always be grateful to have had the opportunity to do.

A couple of years later, Tony Robbins entered my consciousness. A friend has been coaching with him and directed me to his books. This was prior to the world of podcasts and YouTube. Although his ra-ra 'machoness' didn't resonate with me, I saw the benefit, and together with a chiropractic friend, the same one who took me to the UCA conference years ago, we stepped out of our comfort zone and attended one of his live events. There is one word that stands out about that weekend: Intense. No sleep for three days, culminating with a fire walk. We broke some limiting beliefs there!

I've had a few business coaches over the years, each with a different approach, but teaching from a systematic playbook. A couple have also been mentors. One in particular used to ask me to prepare for my sessions; perhaps KPIs on the business or to bring a "problem" I would like her to help solve. Through careful questioning, what I perceived to be the "problem" wasn't really a problem, and the solution was straightforward when I took time to step back and look at it from a different perspective.

Within a clinical setting, and among colleagues I have seen many examples of burnout. People were so obsessed with growing their businesses that they had forgotten to take care of themselves. I didn't want to be someone who forgot to experience the joys of life because I was so focused on a business/financial goal. This observation has definitely guided the direction in which I coach my clients. I take a holistic approach, understanding that health is multifaceted.

I specifically use five pillars of health as a foundation for this approach. This facilitates balance in my life and my clients' lives as a measurement of overall well-being.

As a personal health strategy coach, many clients use our sessions for goal-orientated things. Combining these five pillars of health within personal strategy coaching can contribute to a holistic approach that enhances well-being and achievement in all aspects of a client's life, not just in business.

THE FIVE PILLARS OF HEALTH:

1. Physical Health

Physical well-being provides the energy and vitality needed for sustained focus and productivity. I combine healthy lifestyle strategies, including appropriate exercise, nutrition, and adequate rest.

2. Mindset

A sound mind is crucial for effective decision-making, stress management, and emotional intelligence. I use tried and tested techniques for mental resilience, emotional intelligence, and stress management.

3. Social Health

Building strong social connections is vital for success in various aspects of life. Even introverts need company sometimes. I utilise strategies for effective communication, networking, and relationship-building.

4. Financial Health

Financial stability is a critical component of overall success. Often by setting and achieving financial goals, budgeting, and making strategic financial decisions.

5. Purpose and Fulfilment

Understanding one's purpose and finding fulfilment is crucial for long-term success. Success coaching often delves into helping individuals identify their values, passions, and purpose to guide their personal and professional goals. I use a variety of tools for this.

We often find ourselves engaging in self-sabotage. For example, despite setting financial goals, our lack of financial literacy or tendency to overspend diminishes the likelihood of achieving those targets.

Additionally, ingrained limiting beliefs, often acquired in childhood (such as the notion that one cannot be rich and happy), may hinder our progress. A familiar refrain I frequently heard was 'money doesn't make you happy.' These subconscious beliefs can create internal conflicts, manifesting as subtle self-sabotage where we unconsciously hinder our financial growth, playing a small game without realising the impact of our actions or understanding why we behave how we do. These limiting beliefs are commonly referred to as blocks, and with my holistic approach, I try to find your blind spots, identify where these blocks are, and shine a light on them. I help you process them and release them.

I have included case studies to demonstrate how identifying and releasing a block is crucial if someone is not achieving a desired goal. I am fortunate to offer one sponsored coaching/mentoring slot per year to someone who needs it. It is often in these cases I see the most profound changes. The case below is no exception.

CASE STUDY

Michelle (40) Doula, mother to three neurodivergent children.

I met Michelle at a retreat; we clicked immediately. She is a witty character but lacks confidence and is feeling stuck. She was living in a foreign country where she couldn't work without local qualifications and couldn't speak the language.

Are we a good fit?

We started with a fifteen-minute "good fit" call, where we met and saw if we would work well together. It is essential to build trust early on. I encouraged this by verbalising that our coaching environment is a safe place. With this, and that we had met previously, it took some time to identify the most problematic block. Michelle was feeling trapped. Not only had her marriage "fallen apart", she couldn't travel to see her family as she didn't have a current passport. In order to get a current passport, she needed to have a photo taken. Having had a few health challenges, she was reliant on her husband's income, had no disposable income for herself, and couldn't afford self-care or the fresh food she required. She was isolated in a rural village without transport. Michelle admitted that she had experienced both therapy and coaching before, but she felt talking about her problems hadn't helped.

Using the Pillars of Health as a framework, a quick call enabled me to identify areas to be considered in all five aspects on a biopsychosocial level. If you are familiar with Maslow's Hierarchy of Needs, it was evident that her physiological needs weren't being met. In this state, the sympathetic nervous system shuts down, impacting our thinking and behaviour.

When Michelle's brain went into cloudy mode, the ability to do specific tasks such as critical thinking, problem-solving or finding a way out of our situation went out the window. It was about survival. My primary goal was to reassure her and keep providing her with a safe space. To help her realise that there are different options and ways to do things.

We looked at her current perspective. I drew attention to the feelings of anxiety, loneliness, lethargy and lack of motivation during the session, so I encouraged her to take a step back from the situation and look at it as an outsider. One of the most powerful questions I used that day was, 'If a friend was in your situation, what advice would you give them?' She took a while to think about this and came up with things she would say. We unravelled some thought patterns, and the rest of the session moved smoothly. She made rapid progress following this. Towards the end of the session, I partnered with Michelle to set an accountability deadline to get the photo done.

By this time, it was apparent that she couldn't afford to pay for coaching. But I could see she was struggling—a feeling I understood well. When I was at university, it was financially and emotionally challenging. A kind couple introduced me to the "paying it forward" approach. In simple terms, this means when someone does something for you, instead of paying that person back directly, you pass it on to another person when you can. I was in a position to help Michelle, so I chose to gift her some sessions.

Michelle surpassed the deadline, and within twenty-four hours, I received a message to say that she had not only got the headshot done but also sent the whole application off to the passport agency, something she had struggled to do for the last year!

In our subsequent session, Michelle expressed concern that I might always assign tasks during our conversations. I promptly reassured her that each session was tailored to her needs and I would not introduce any homework without her consent. And this is something I have found has also put me off coaching – knowing that I need to get tasks done to "make the coach happy". This was a good reminder to me to improve my technique as a coach – allowing sessions to be fully client-led and that setting goals can also me a cause of stress. During this session, it became apparent that her current domestic situation wasn't fulfilling her needs, prompting a discussion about potential solutions. Michelle made adjustments to provide everyone in the family home with the space to be alone. Also, a significant moment occurred when she received her passport, expressing newfound joy and a sense of having choices.

We initiated our work with an exercise known as the Wheel of Life, a process that helped pinpoint crucial areas for improvement. For seven weekly calls, we systematically addressed these areas. While not every session was goal-oriented, our collaborative efforts led to tangible changes in Michelle's living arrangements, improved routines, and overall stability.

Communication within her household witnessed enhancements, resulting in fewer meltdowns. Concurrently, Michelle diligently worked on boosting her confidence.

Having navigated a challenging upbringing in a cult, Michelle successfully reframed some limiting beliefs, shifting her focus towards her strengths and emphasising what she can do rather than dwelling on limitations. In a recent check-in, Michelle enthusiastically reported securing a position as a writer for a local expat newspaper, sharing her experiences living abroad. She attends language school part-time and contributes to the local council, ensuring a steady income. Her husband also holds a stable job. Looking ahead, Michelle envisions expanding her doula business to support more families through the birth process, with the bonus of her unused passport awaiting future adventures.

Michelle's thoughts:

'I have had seven sessions with the kind and generous Mary. Our discovery call back in March inspired me to take a seemingly small step in finally getting something done that I had been procrastinating on for one year. Together, we set an achievable goal, which I quickly smashed, and I knew then that our time together would be life-changing. Mary's support on that fifteen-minute call truly was a catalyst for a deep transformation in my life! That initial momentum has been built upon with each session, and the ongoing transformation in my life has me totally buzzing!'

Takeaway:

Collaborating with Michelle was a humbling experience for me. I'm accustomed to working with busy clinicians and entrepreneurs who generally have a clear direction but may need help introducing systems, discussing their thoughts, or finding a balance in their lives. It served as a poignant reminder that seeking assistance can be challenging. This has heightened my awareness of offering appropriate support, and I continue to provide coaching whenever possible. Michelle's situation underscores the need for connection and the importance of being heard. It also emphasises the crucial role of mindset; our thoughts can either propel us forward or hold us back. Some personalities are more prone to overthinking, which is acceptable if they follow it with decisive action. However, failing to translate our thoughts into action poses the risk of maintaining the status quo.

Coaching has been instrumental in revealing that I benefit from verbalising to process my thoughts. Growing up in a household with four children, usually, it was the loudest voice that received attention. Bickering was a way of communication. Consequently, I had to unlearn ingrained habits, like believing I had to do it myself for something to be done correctly. Engaging with a coach provided me with valuable time and space to articulate my thoughts and recognise that I cannot accomplish everything to the desired standard. I've come to appreciate that sometimes finishing a project is better than it not being done at all, and there are skills at which others excel more than I do. I'm naturally curious, and coaching fuels this curiosity.

Wanting to spend more time with my family, who are dotted all over Europe, made coaching a good career option. It complimented what I was doing in the clinic and gave me more flexibility to work worldwide. My unquenchable thirst for knowledge inspired me to take a few courses to hone my skills. Having worked in the private health sector for over two decades, I mentored new graduates. When COVID-19 occurred, and many practitioners could no longer work face-to-face with patients, I volunteered to help some struggling newcomers into our profession. I put into practice things I had learned as a coach and mentee, and as time passed, I saw the ripple effect of lives changing from what we were doing. I am an eternal student and decided to undertake an accredited qualification to help me become an even better coach.

I have had the opportunity to work with a diverse mix of people over the years. When someone engages a coach, they often have no idea what to expect. They've realised something isn't quite right with an aspect of their world. Quite often, they can't even put their finger on it. They just know there is a discord. The coach then helps them explore what's happening and what they want to change.

Like everything, there is a process, and depending on how deep the client wants to go, making lasting changes can take a minimum of twelve weeks to implement. Otherwise, it could turn into a temporary fix without a long-term solution. I like to refer to this as a "jacuzzi experience." If habits don't change, we return to our ingrained nature and repeat the same patterns. When we repeat the same patterns, we tend to get the same results; funny, eh?

Coaching helps us understand where our patterns come from, to see things from a different perspective and allow ourselves permission to change these – if they want to. It can be daunting and take many years to change habits we have carried since childhood. It has made me more aware of my actions as a parent. I am more easy-going, opting for informed discussions, rather than the dictatorial upbringing I experienced.

CASE STUDY

Carys (37) is a solo parent of two children.

During the challenging days of the first lockdown, Carys, a chiropractor managing two clinics, crossed paths with me. With a demanding chiropractic schedule and unexpected time on my hands, I extended complimentary coaching sessions to give back to the profession. Carys, facing the complexities of being a self-employed associate with a high-needs autistic son, responded to the lifeline. Little did we know that this encounter would lead to a transformative journey encompassing the interconnected pillars of health—mindset, physical, social, financial, and purposeful fulfilment.

Carys, also dealing with the departure of her children's father and ensuing debt, became the focus of our initial coaching sessions. We addressed disrupted sleep, familial disputes, and financial constraints collaboratively—the plan aimed to secure additional support for her children and alleviate the constant household pressure on Carys.

As our strategic interventions unfolded, Carys's family dynamic took centre stage, exposing a complex relationship with her parents. Despite being adults living under the same roof, she saw her parents treating her like a child. Transactional Analysis (TA) sheds light on this unhealthy dynamic, exploring the three ego states: Parent, Adult, and Child.

Tensions peaked as Carys spontaneously bought a larger house with her parents, seeking family equality. Months later, she contemplated the daunting decision of living separately for independence. Drawing on my business coaching experience, I connected her with resources to navigate mortgage intricacies. Carys made a pivotal decision—to establish her own business.

We meticulously crafted a comprehensive business plan, seeking grants and building an impressive client base.

The turning point came with a devised plan for Carys to break the familial mould by moving out of the jointly purchased house. After eighteen months of relentless effort, she saved enough for a mortgage deposit, marking a new chapter miles away from her parents. In this three-year journey I was privileged to witness remarkable milestones—Carys purchased her own house, established her clinic, achieved financial stability, and crystallised a clear vision for her life.

Evolving from a coaching relationship to a mentorship, our sessions delved into case discussions, addressing industry-specific challenges, problem-solving, and prioritising Carys's health amid overwhelming situations. Carys's story stands as a testament to growth, resilience, and the profound impact of strategic support across the interconnected pillars of health. It encourages reflection on the transformative power of mentorship and determination in crafting a fulfilling and balanced life.

Takeaway:

While challenges are inevitable, Carys's ongoing self-awareness promises to unveil untapped potential within herself, reflecting the untapped potential we all hold across the dimensions of mindset, physical, social, financial, and purposeful fulfilment. I've seen her grow and watched how her confidence has changed and now she passes the ripple effect through her community.

CASE STUDY

Ruth (55) is single with two grown-up children living at home.

Ruth's journey highlights the interconnected nature of life challenges. It demonstrates that issues in business, personal well-being, and financial obligations are often intertwined. Addressing one aspect can have a positive ripple effect on others.

Introduced to Ruth through a former colleague, I discovered she was undergoing aggressive mentoring, causing overwhelm in deciding the best course of action for her businesses. Doubting her capabilities, she even contemplated selling two of her most profitable chains to a local businessman.

Becoming Ruth's sounding board, I introduced her to the concept of the Wheel of Life—a powerful tool that could provide clarity and guide her towards balance. This tool, reflecting the pillars of health, became instrumental in identifying areas for improvement, especially considering the challenges of menopause and the weight of financial obligations, including significant debt from buying the businesses.

As Ruth navigated the challenges of running her businesses, managing clinicians, and grappling with the impact of menopause, the Wheel of Life allowed her to assess critical aspects, such as business, health, relationships, and self-care. This holistic approach unveiled a comprehensive view of her life, prompting reflection on areas that needed attention.

Beyond the business intricacies, Ruth recognised the importance of addressing her well-being, especially amidst the mental strain of significant debt. The Wheel of Life became a compass, guiding Ruth to focus on self-care, navigate self-doubt, and make informed decisions, not only for her businesses but also for her overall health and financial stability.

Our collaborative efforts, fuelled by insights from the Wheel of Life, centred on a balanced approach to life's complexities. Ruth's journey exemplifies the transformative power of this tool, helping her navigate decision-making for her own health, manage self-doubt, and find equilibrium in the pillars of health and financial obligations—ultimately contributing to her overall well-being and success.

When this is also balanced, there is this equilibrium. I use this model to coach to ensure that all aspects of a person are balanced so that we are whole. There will always be times when we feel out of balance, but if we can identify whether is occurring and why, we can get back on track faster and begin to feel more like ourselves. This is a great self-coaching tool you can use at home. I like to do it at least a couple of times a year to reassess where I am at.

Takeaway:

Reflecting on Ruth's transformative journey, there's a powerful reminder that life's challenges, whether in business, personal well-being, or financial obligations, are interconnected. Introducing the Wheel of Life as a guiding compass allowed Ruth to navigate the complexities of her companies and shed light on neglected aspects of her life, particularly during the challenging phases of menopause and significant financial strain. This narrative serves as a poignant reflection for readers, underscoring the importance of holistic approaches to problem-solving and decision-making. It prompts contemplation on how tools like the Wheel of Life can offer clarity, guiding us toward a balanced perspective that encompasses professional success, personal well-being, and financial stability. Ruth's story becomes an inspiring testament to the potential for transformative growth when we acknowledge and address the various facets of our lives.

In the intricate tapestry of coaching, the unpredictability of each session adds a layer of excitement and mystery, reminiscent of my teenage days shelving books in a library. Just as I discovered the power of personal development books during those repetitive tasks, coaching sessions unfold with the promise of transformative insights and life-altering decisions.

From setting goals after graduation to attending conferences and exploring various coaching approaches, my journey mirrors the evolution of coaching itself. The introduction of the Wheel of Life, grounded in the five pillars of health, became a compass to guide clients like Ruth and Michelle through the complexities of their lives. These case studies vividly illustrate how addressing physical, mental, social, financial, and purposeful aspects contributes to a holistic approach, fostering well-being and achievement.

Michelle's journey, marked by isolation, financial struggles, and a lack of direction, exemplifies the profound impact coaching can have on one's life. Utilising the Pillars of Health, we navigated through her challenges, unlocking a transformation that rippled through various facets, from improved family dynamics to newfound professional opportunities. Ruth's case, grappling with aggressive mentoring, self-doubt, and significant financial obligations, delved into the power of the Wheel of Life. This tool guided her in business decisions and prompted a reflection on neglected areas of her life, ultimately leading to a more balanced and fulfilling existence.

As a coach, my role extends beyond the professional realm. Carys's journey, intertwined with family dynamics, business success, and personal growth, showcases the mentorship aspect of coaching. Evolving from a coach to a mentor, our collaborative sessions tackled industry challenges, problem-solving, and prioritising health, resulting in remarkable milestones over three years.

Reflecting on these transformative journeys, coaching emerges as a process and a catalyst for profound change. Each case study is a testament to the interconnectedness of life's challenges and the importance of holistically addressing them. The pillars of health are a foundation to build from and can be combined with The Wheel of Life so it becomes more than a tool; it becomes a guiding philosophy, encouraging readers to contemplate their balance across the pillars of health.

Coaching is a journey of self-discovery, a narrative woven with diverse threads of challenges, growth, and resilience. Like I once devoured personal development books, coaching unfolds the pages of individuals' lives, offering the promise of a different destiny—one where the power to create change lies within, waiting to be unlocked through intentional and transformative conversations.

I feel blessed to come from a health background and can now help even more people understand and experience a deeper level of cohesiveness, and acknowledge that asking for help isn't weakness. I would love everyone to experience coaching with a qualified coach they trust. My personal mission is to serve and to help as many people as possible to become the best version of themselves by asking those tricky questions so that their dreams and aspirations become their reality, whatever those dreams may be.

ABOUT MARY PHILLIPS

Mary is a personal health strategist coach who helps people in midlife get more balance in their lives. She graduated as a Doctor of Chiropractic in 2005 and through this training she is uniquely equipped with diverse skills from running businesses to managing people's holistic health to creating meditations for peak performance and public speaking.

Before Mary began coaching she spent fifteen years mentoring clinics in the UK as well as building her own businesses, both online and in bricks and mortar.

She believes life should be fun and we all deserve to have the skills to live a life we love.

Mary loves to spend time in nature. She particularly enjoys sunshine, good food, travelling, riding her motorbike and spending quality time with her favourite people.

Mary is available for coaching and for speaking engagements.

You can reach Mary at:

Email: hello@consciousbutterfly.co.uk
Website (coaching): www.maryphillips.co.uk
Website (meditations): www.consciousbutterfly.co.uk

facebook.com/consciousbutterfly
instagram.com/drmary_phillips

9

AMPLIFYING VOICES: "IF YOU CAN'T SEE IT, YOU CAN'T BE IT" — METRA ROWE

THE IMPERATIVE OF COACHES FROM UNDERREPRESENTED BACKGROUNDS IN DIVERSITY, EQUITY, AND INCLUSION (DEI) COACHING

In the ever-evolving landscape of the modern workplace and society, I have witnessed first-hand, how the principles of Diversity, Equity, and Inclusion (DEI) have emerged as pivotal factors in shaping organisational success and societal progress. As organisations strive to create diverse and inclusive environments, DEI coaching has gained prominence as a crucial tool in navigating the complexities of this transformative journey. What strikes me as particularly significant is the need for the active participation of coaches who themselves hail from underrepresented backgrounds. In this chapter, I will delve into the compelling reasons behind this imperative, highlighting how coaches from underrepresented backgrounds, like myself, bring unique perspectives, authenticity, and expertise that can drive profound change within individuals, organisations, and communities.

THE EVOLVING LANDSCAPE OF DEI

Before delving into the importance of coaches from underrepresented backgrounds in DEI coaching, it is vital to understand the broader context in which diversity, equity, and inclusion have gained prominence in contemporary workplaces and society. DEI has transitioned from a mere buzzword to a fundamental pillar of organisational culture and societal progress, driven by a combination of factors, ranging from business imperatives to ethical considerations. Organisations that recognise and embrace these reasons are better positioned to thrive in a rapidly changing world.

Leading Innovation and Creativity

Diverse perspectives inherently fuel innovation and creativity. When individuals from various backgrounds collaborate, they bring together a rich tapestry of ideas, experiences, and insights. This synergy leads to innovative solutions and helps organisations adapt to an ever-changing world.

Meeting Market Demands

In today's globalised and interconnected world, consumers and clients demand products and services that reflect the diversity of their communities. Organisations that embrace diversity are better positioned to meet these demands and stay competitive.

Legal and Ethical Obligations

Legislation and ethical considerations have made it clear that discrimination and exclusion are unacceptable. Organisations are legally obligated to promote diversity and ensure equitable treatment for all employees.

Employee Wellbeing and Productivity

Inclusive workplaces contribute to higher levels of employee well-being and satisfaction, ultimately boosting productivity. Employees who feel valued and included are more likely to give their best to the organisation.

Globalisation and Cross-cultural Collaboration

As businesses expand globally, they increasingly interact with diverse cultures and markets. Having a diverse and culturally competent workforce is essential for effective cross-cultural communication and collaboration.

Demographic Shifts

In many countries, demographic changes are leading to more diverse populations. To attract and retain top talent, organisations must reflect the demographics of the communities they serve.

Ethical and Moral Imperatives

There is a growing recognition that promoting diversity and inclusion is a matter of ethics and morality. It aligns with the principles of fairness, equality, and social justice, which resonate with employees, customers, and society at large.

Enhancing Reputation

Organisations that actively promote DEI are seen as socially responsible and ethical entities. This positive reputation can attract customers, investors, and top talent, further contributing to success.

Reducing Bias and Stereotypes

DEI initiatives help challenge biases and stereotypes within organisations. This leads to fairer decision-making processes, including in hiring, promotions, and resource allocation.

Strengthening Employee Engagement

Inclusive workplaces foster a sense of belonging and psychological safety. This, in turn, leads to higher levels of employee engagement, which positively impacts retention rates and organisational performance.

Promoting Social Progress

Beyond the workplace, DEI initiatives contribute to broader societal progress by challenging systemic inequalities and promoting social cohesion.

THE ROLE OF DEI COACHING – IT'S A JOURNEY, NOT A DESTINATION!

It's almost certain that your organisation is increasingly recognising the significance of DEI, and you find yourselves facing a complex landscape when it comes to implementing and sustaining these principles in the workplace. Firstly, let me say this is not unusual! You should take comfort in knowing a great many organisations start at the same point, regardless of their size and scale. The task of promoting diversity, ensuring equity, and fostering inclusion isn't just a one-off effort; it's an ongoing journey that demands careful planning, continuous learning, and a deep commitment to change. Secondly, I'd commend you on acknowledging these challenges, and encourage you to actively seek guidance and support from those experienced in this field, to navigate this intricate terrain.

So, in response to your growing need, you'll likely begin with education and exposure to the topic. Alongside this, you could look at DEI coaching, which has risen to prominence as an invaluable resource over the last few years. It has become an indispensable tool that provides individuals and organisations with the essential guidance and strategies required to successfully move towards a more inclusive culture and working environment. DEI coaches serve as trusted partners in this journey, helping individuals and organisations develop the awareness, understanding, behaviours, skills, and knowledge necessary to navigate the complexities of diversity, equity, and inclusion.

What is DEI Coaching?

DEI coaching is a dynamic process that involves individual or group coaching sessions aimed at promoting diversity, equity, and inclusion within an organisation. Coaches work closely with individuals, teams, and leaders to develop awareness, empathy, and actionable strategies to develop an inclusive environment.

DEI coaching operates on multiple levels within organisations. It provides leaders and managers with the tools to create inclusive workplaces where all employees can thrive. It empowers employees to recognise and challenge biases, fostering a culture of respect and understanding. DEI coaching also helps organisations design and implement DEI initiatives and programmes that are tailored to their unique needs and challenges, ensuring they are effective and sustainable.

Furthermore, DEI coaching encourages open and honest conversations about diversity, inclusion, and belonging, which can be uncomfortable but are essential for growth. It creates a safe space for individuals to explore their own biases, assumptions, and blind spots, facilitating personal and professional development.

The Need for DEI Coaching

While the commitment to DEI is essential, it can be challenging to navigate without expert guidance. DEI coaches play a pivotal role in facilitating conversations, addressing biases, and guiding organisations in creating lasting change. Their expertise bridges the gap between intention and implementation.

DEI coaching has emerged as an indispensable resource for organisations on their journey to creating diverse, equitable and inclusive environments. By providing guidance, support and a safe space for learning and growth, DEI coaching plays a vital role in helping individuals and organisations navigate the complexities of this transformative journey. It is an investment that not only benefits the organisation but also contributes to the broader goal of building a more inclusive and just society.

Within the realm of DEI coaching, the inclusion of coaches from underrepresented backgrounds has emerged as a critical imperative. These coaches bring a unique set of qualities and experiences that can profoundly impact individuals, organisations, and communities.

REASONS WHY ORGANISATIONS INVEST IN DEI COACHING PROGRAMMES

Exploring the world of Diversity, Equity, and Inclusion (DEI) can benefit everyone, but DEI coaching programs offer particular value in certain situations and here's the reason why you or your organisation might want to consider it:

If your goal is to lead and nurture an inclusive workplace culture where everyone, regardless of their background, feels genuinely welcomed, DEI coaching programmes are a powerful resource. Coaches specialising in diversity and inclusion can help develop strategies and initiatives tailored to your organisation's unique needs. They can guide you in implementing practices that go beyond superficial diversity, fostering a sense of belonging and equitable treatment for all employees.

Individuals who identify with traditionally oppressed identities and encounter difficulties in feeling a sense of belonging or confidence in their workplace can greatly benefit from DEI coaching. A DEI coach can provide vital support by assisting them in reflecting on their identities, identifying their strengths and talents, and helping them build self-confidence.

Yes, your organisations and leaders indeed play a pivotal role in promoting diversity, equity, and inclusion, but it's not enough to simply aim for diversity in hiring; your organisation must actively strive to create an equitable and inclusive culture. While the process of cultivating an inclusive workplace culture can be nuanced and complex, well-established DEI strategies, such as mandatory leadership development, the establishment of inclusion councils, and the implementation of various DEI learning approaches including DEI development, can propel your organisation forward.

Considering DEI coaching programmes is a strategic decision for those looking to deepen their commitment to DEI principles. It represents an investment in personal and professional growth, as well as a commitment to creating more equitable and inclusive environments where every individual can thrive. By engaging with a DEI coach, organisations allow their employees to embark on a journey of self-discovery, empathy building, and cultural transformation that ultimately benefits both the individuals and the broader community.

WHY WE NEED TO INCREASE THE NUMBER OF COACHES FROM UNDER-REPRESENTED BACKGROUNDS

Representation Matters

Coaches from underrepresented backgrounds possess first-hand experience with the challenges and barriers that marginalised groups face. Their presence as coaches not only provides visibility and representation but also underscores the possibility of achieving success despite adversity. When individuals see coaches who share their background succeeding, they are more likely to feel inspired and empowered to pursue their own goals.

Cultural Competence

Coaches from underrepresented backgrounds are often more attuned to the cultural nuances and sensitivities related to diversity and inclusion. This heightened cultural competence enables them to engage in more meaningful conversations and exercises, creating a safe space where clients can openly discuss their experiences, concerns, and aspirations. This, in turn, enhances the effectiveness of DEI coaching.

Relatability and Trust

Building trust between a coach and their client is essential for effective coaching outcomes. Coaches from underrepresented backgrounds often have shared experiences, enabling them to establish rapport quickly and more deeply. Clients may feel more comfortable discussing their challenges and seeking guidance from coaches who have navigated similar paths, leading to more impactful coaching relationships.

Authenticity and Empathy

The authentic stories and empathy that coaches from underrepresented backgrounds bring to their coaching practice create a more empathetic and supportive environment. Clients feel understood and validated when their coaches can draw on personal experiences to provide context and insights. This authenticity provides an atmosphere of genuine care and respect, driving clients' commitment to personal growth.

Breaking Stereotypes

Coaches from underrepresented backgrounds challenge stereotypes and biases by showcasing their expertise and knowledge in coaching. By excelling in their roles, they defy limiting perceptions and demonstrate that talent, competence, and leadership can transcend traditional boundaries. This not only benefits clients but also contributes to the broader cultural shift towards breaking down barriers.

Addressing Intersectionality

Many individuals belong to multiple underrepresented groups, which can lead to unique challenges at the intersection of these identities. Coaches from underrepresented backgrounds are better equipped to understand and address these complexities, providing more comprehensive support and tailored strategies that account for the diverse layers of a client's identity.

Overall, the involvement of coaches from underrepresented backgrounds in delivering DEI coaching is pivotal in driving meaningful change within individuals and organisations. Their lived experiences, cultural insights, and empathetic approach enable them to connect deeply with clients, driving more effective learning and growth. As the world continues to prioritise diversity, equality, and inclusion, the contributions of coaches from underrepresented backgrounds are essential in creating a more just, equitable, and inclusive society.

HOW THE RIGHT COACHING FROM THE RIGHT PERSON CAN MAKE ALL THE DIFFERENCE

CASE STUDY ONE

Background

Marwah, a skilled professional from a Middle Eastern background, had been working in a large corporate organisation for several years. While she was highly skilled and experienced in her role, she often felt like she was facing unique challenges related to her background. These challenges included subtle biases, a lack of representation in leadership, and difficulties in navigating the corporate culture. Marwah was ambitious and determined to succeed, but she felt that she needed guidance and support tailored to her specific situation.

The Coaching Experience

Marwah's organisation recognised the importance of diversity and had recently introduced a DEI coaching programme. They matched Marwah with Amira, a seasoned DEI coach who not only had extensive experience but also came from a similar underrepresented background. This pairing aimed to provide Marwah with the support and guidance she needed, knowing that Amira's shared experiences would make a significant difference.

During their coaching sessions, Amira and Marwah had open and candid conversations about the challenges Marwah faced in the workplace. Amira's unique perspective as someone who had also encountered similar obstacles allowed her to empathise with Marwah's experiences deeply. They discussed issues such as navigating microaggressions, building a professional network, and overcoming imposter syndrome, all of which were specific to Marwah's background.

Amira used a combination of coaching techniques, including active listening, questioning, and goal setting, to help Marwah gain clarity on her career aspirations and develop strategies to overcome barriers. They worked together to set actionable goals and create a personalised plan for Marwah's professional growth.

Why It Worked

Several factors contributed to the success of this coaching relationship:

- Amira's shared background with Marwah created an immediate sense of trust and understanding. Marwah felt comfortable discussing her challenges openly, knowing that Amira could relate.
- Amira's ability to tailor her coaching approach to Marwah's unique needs and experiences ensured that the coaching was highly relevant and impactful.
- Through coaching, Marwah felt empowered to address the challenges she faced head-on. She gained confidence and a renewed sense of purpose in her career.
- The structured coaching process held Marwah accountable for her goals, ensuring that she made tangible progress.

The Outcome

Throughout the coaching engagement, Marwah made significant strides in her career. She not only developed a stronger sense of self-confidence but also honed her networking and communication skills. Amira's guidance helped her navigate workplace challenges more effectively, and she was promoted to a leadership position within her organisation.

Furthermore, the success of Marwah's coaching experience highlighted the value of coaches from underrepresented backgrounds in DEI initiatives within the organisation. It inspired similar coaching relationships and contributed to a more inclusive workplace culture. Marwah's journey demonstrated that with the right support and guidance, individuals from under-represented backgrounds can overcome obstacles and achieve their career aspirations, ultimately contributing to the organisation's success and diversity goals.

CASE STUDY TWO

Background

A renowned UK university, embarked on a mission to enhance its support for students with disabilities, ensuring their full participation in campus life. Recognising the need for a comprehensive approach, they launched the 'Access Ability' coach initiative, promoting disability inclusion in higher education. This ground-breaking programme aimed to empower disabled students by enlisting coaches who themselves had disabilities and had successfully navigated academia and beyond. These coaches would provide DEI coaching, addressing critical issues such as self-advocacy, accommodations, and post-graduation transitions.

Why It Worked

The 'Access Ability' coach initiative's success was deeply rooted in several key factors:

- Coaches with disabilities brought a profound understanding of the challenges faced by disabled students. Their shared experiences created an immediate bond of trust and relatability, allowing students to open up and seek guidance comfortably.
- These coaches provided practical advice and emotional support that was uniquely tailored to the student's specific challenges. Their insights were informed by

personal experiences, making their guidance exceptionally relevant and effective.
- The coaches were attuned to the cultural and societal nuances of the UK context, ensuring that their coaching was culturally sensitive and aligned with the needs of the students.
- The authenticity of the coaches was a driving force in building students' self-esteem and confidence. They served as inspiring role models, showing that disability need not be a barrier to success.

What Happened

Through the 'Access Ability' coach initiative, disabled students at the university gained access to a supportive network of coaches who understood their unique journey. These coaches conducted one-to-one coaching sessions, addressing a range of topics, from self-advocacy skills to navigating accommodations and preparing for life after graduation.

Students reported profound improvements in their self-esteem, academic performance, and engagement in extracurricular activities. The coaches' guidance and mentorship went beyond academics, helping students develop essential life skills and prepare for a successful transition into the workforce.

The Outcome

The impact of the initiative was remarkable. The university witnessed a substantial increase in the retention and graduation rates of disabled students. This indicated that the 'Access Ability' coach initiative had successfully developed a more inclusive and accessible learning environment.

Moreover, the initiative served as a powerful testament to the potential of coaches from underrepresented backgrounds in facilitating meaningful change. By empowering disabled students with the support, they needed, the university not only improved individual outcomes but also contributed to a more inclusive society, where individuals from diverse backgrounds could thrive and succeed.

WHY DEI COACHING PROGRAMMES MATTER MORE THAN EVER AND *HOW* THEY MAKE A DIFFERENCE

In addition to driving innovation, competitiveness, and better decision-making, prioritising DEI coaching programmes is crucial to driving employee engagement and retention.

- 55% of HR professionals say that promoting diversity, equity and inclusion is a top priority for their organisation.*
- Organisations that prioritise DEI are six times more likely to be innovative and agile, and twice as likely to meet or exceed financial targets.**
- 76% of job seekers and employees consider an organisation's diversity and inclusion when deciding where to apply for jobs.***

** SHRM 2021 ** Accenture 2019 *** Glassdoor 2021*

CULTIVATING A CULTURE OF INCLUSIVITY AND EMPOWERMENT IN THE WORKPLACE

Creating a collaborative and productive workplace harnesses the wealth of diverse perspectives and experiences among your employees. This approach ultimately enhances decision-making and contributes to improved long-term business outcomes.

- 61% of employees have witnessed or experienced discrimination at work, and 57% believe their company should do more to increase diversity.*
- 72% of employees believe their organisation should be doing more to foster an inclusive culture.**
- While 74% of organisations have DEI initiatives, only 32% have metrics in place to measure the effectiveness of those initiatives.***

** Glassdoor – 2021 ** Deloitte 2020 *** SHRM 2020*

HELPING EVERYONE TO GET "COMFORTABLE WITH BEING UNCOMFORTABLE"

This is a powerful concept that underpins the importance of embracing change, taking risks, and navigating unfamiliar territory for you or your organisation. It involves encouraging everyone to step outside their comfort zones, confront challenges, and push boundaries to achieve personal and organisational growth.

You and those in your organisation will often find yourselves in situations where you need to adapt to new circumstances, technologies, or market conditions. Getting comfortable with being uncomfortable means accepting that change is a constant part of the modern workplace and that it can lead to valuable learning experiences through a growth mindset.

This type of growth mindset often requires making bold decisions and taking calculated risks. When you are willing to step out of your comfort zone, you are more likely to innovate and explore new opportunities, even if it involves uncertainty.

Stepping into the unknown can be challenging, but it also offers significant opportunities for personal and professional growth for you and your organisation. When you embrace discomfort, you are more likely to acquire new skills, broaden your perspectives, and develop resilience in the face of adversity.

Encouraging those around you to get comfortable with being uncomfortable can also improve everyone's communication skills. It enables you all to have difficult conversations, address conflicts, and engage in constructive feedback, all of which are essential for effective relationships.

In the context of diversity and inclusion, when you embrace discomfort you are more likely to create inclusive environments where diverse perspectives are valued. You are open to acknowledging and addressing biases, fostering greater equity, and ensuring that everyone has a voice.

Innovation often arises from challenging the status quo and exploring uncharted territory. When you are comfortable with discomfort, you can inspire creativity and innovation within your teams and organisations.

Finally, getting comfortable with being uncomfortable can build resilience. Learning to navigate uncertainty, setbacks, and adversity with greater composure and determination, can ultimately make you more effective in your role.

In summary, helping everyone become comfortable with discomfort is about encouraging them to embrace change, take risks, and push their boundaries. It is a mindset that fosters learning, growth, innovation, and resilience, ultimately contributing to effective relationships and organisational success.

- 88% of coachees believe coaching helps leaders to develop DEI skills.*
- 55% of organisations reported increased awareness and understanding of DEI issues as a result of coaching.**
- 79% of coachees believe coaching helps leaders to create a more inclusive workplace culture.*

* International Coaching Federation – 2020 **HCI 2019

WHAT A DEI COACHING PROGRAMME INCLUDES

A typical Diversity, Equity, and Inclusion (DEI) coaching programme is designed to help individuals and organisations develop a deeper understanding of DEI principles, foster inclusive practices, and drive positive change. While the specific components of DEI coaching programmes can vary, here are some common elements you might find in such a programme:

Assessment and Goal Setting

A DEI coaching programme often commences with a thorough assessment of the current DEI landscape within an organisation or an individual's level of DEI awareness and understanding. Through surveys, interviews, or self-assessment tools, coaches gain insight into the existing strengths and challenges. Based on this assessment, specific goals and objectives are set for the coaching engagement. These goals serve as a roadmap for the entire programme.

Education and Training

A fundamental component of DEI coaching is education and training. This can take various forms, such as workshops, seminars, webinars, or online courses. Participants are provided with foundational knowledge about DEI concepts and principles. Topics may include understanding unconscious bias, recognising privilege, addressing microaggressions, and developing cultural competency. This educational component equips individuals with the vocabulary and frameworks needed to engage effectively in DEI discussions.

Individual Coaching Sessions

One-to-one coaching sessions are at the heart of DEI coaching. Coaches work closely with participants, whether they are individuals seeking personal growth or organisations aiming to embed DEI principles. These sessions provide a safe and confidential space for participants to explore their personal biases, challenges, and opportunities for growth. Coaches use active listening, probing questions, and constructive feedback to help individuals navigate DEI issues specific to their context. These sessions are highly personalised to address the unique needs and circumstances of each participant.

Group Coaching and Facilitation

Some DEI coaching programmes incorporate group coaching or facilitation sessions. These group dynamics encourage open dialogue, the sharing of experiences, and collaborative problem-solving. Participants can learn from each other's perspectives and build a sense of collective responsibility for DEI goals. Group coaching fosters a sense of community and mutual support.

Skill Building and Action-Planning

DEI coaching helps individuals and organisations translate knowledge into action. Coaches assist participants in developing practical skills and creating actionable plans. These plans may encompass strategies for building inclusive teams, addressing biases in decision-making processes, and promoting diversity and equity in hiring and promotion practices. Participants are encouraged to set specific, measurable, achievable, relevant, and time-bound (SMART) goals.

Feedback and Reflection

Constructive feedback is a vital element of DEI coaching. Coaches provide feedback on participants' behaviour, communication, and actions related to DEI. This feedback helps individuals identify areas for improvement and self-awareness. Reflective exercises and self-assessment tools encourage participants to examine their own biases, behaviours, and contributions to creating an inclusive environment.

Measuring Progress

DEI coaching programmes often emphasise the importance of tracking progress. Coaches and participants establish checkpoints and key performance indicators to measure progress toward established DEI goals. Regular assessments and feedback loops ensure that DEI initiatives are making a positive impact and help in adjusting strategies as needed.

Resource and Tool Access

Coaches may provide access to a wealth of DEI resources, toolkits, literature, and best practices. These resources serve as references and guides for ongoing learning and development. Participants are encouraged to explore additional materials to deepen their understanding of DEI.

Cultural Competency and Awareness

DEI coaching frequently focuses on developing cultural competency and awareness. Participants explore different cultures, identities, and experiences to build empathy and understanding. Coaches facilitate discussions and activities that promote cultural sensitivity and competence.

Sustainability and Integration

Effective DEI coaching programmes emphasise the long-term sustainability of DEI initiatives. Coaches work closely with individuals and organisations to ensure that DEI practices become integrated into everyday operations and organisational culture. This involves embedding DEI principles into policies, procedures, and decision-making processes.

Accountability

Accountability is a fundamental aspect of DEI coaching. Coaches help participants stay accountable for their DEI commitments and goals. Regular progress assessments and accountability check-ins ensure that participants remain on track and continuously strive toward their DEI objectives.

Continuous Learning

DEI coaching is often viewed as an ongoing journey. Participants are encouraged to maintain a commitment to continuous learning and evolution of their DEI strategies. Staying up-to-date with emerging DEI trends and best practices is essential for staying effective in fostering diversity, equity, and inclusion.

I'll conclude by saying that a comprehensive DEI coaching programme would offer a holistic approach to advancing diversity, equity, and inclusion for you and your organisation. It combines education, self-awareness, skill-building, and practical action to help you drive meaningful and sustainable change. The flexibility to tailor the programme to specific needs and goals ensures that you receive targeted support to address the unique challenges and opportunities you encounter on your DEI journey.

It is also important to note that DEI coaches from underrepresented groups play a pivotal role in ensuring success. It is crucial to acknowledge that the specific structure and content of DEI coaching programmes can vary widely based on the goals, needs, and context. Customisation, especially with the guidance of DEI coaches from underrepresented backgrounds, is essential for effectively addressing the unique challenges and opportunities related to diversity, equity, and inclusion that you or your organisation may encounter.

Embrace this approach, and you **will** embark on a journey toward creating a vibrant and inclusive workplace where **everyone** truly feels like they belong; somewhere everyone has a chance to be the best version of themselves. After all, as the title of my chapter suggests *"If you can't see it – you can't be it!"*

References:

SHRM 2020 / 2021
Accenture 2019
Glassdoor 2021
Deloitte 2020
International Coaching Federation – 2020
HCI 2019

ABOUT METRA ROWE

Metra Rowe is an organisation change and development leader experienced in delivering people, business transformation and inclusive culture change at global levels for over twenty years.

As a Professional Certified Coach specialising in DEI, Metra is passionate about making workplaces fair and supportive, ensuring everyone feels like they belong. She thinks this is essential for any organisation to succeed, perform well, and last over time, and with the help of her team of Associate Partners (all skilled practitioners and qualified coaches) and the provisions of her consultancy 'Starling Business Solutions', she believes this success is within the grasp of every organisation.

Metra also believes this approach should be carefully planned and monitored, with responsibility starting from the top leadership and following through with behaviour change.

Alongside her consultancy business, Metra focuses her efforts on hosting guest lectures and workshops as an equity, diversity, and inclusion activist as a co-founder of #spacetotalk; which is a DEI initiative focused on creating a better place to work and live for the future generations, providing pastoral support, information, and guidance). She is also the chair of the DEI board for Nottingham Forest Football Club Community Trust.

When Metra isn't working, she pursues her passion for exploring new cultures through travel and learning new languages.

Website: https://starlingbusinesssolutions.com/
Email: metra@wearestarling.co

instagram.com/wearestarling
linkedin.com/in/metrarowe

10

BIG CHANGES THROUGH COACHING SMALL BUSINESSES — MORTEN ISNES

"We never know how far-reaching something we may think, say or do today will affect the lives of millions tomorrow"

— B.J. PALMER

We rarely know just how much we might be helping people. This is especially true as coaches, and it is something we perhaps only realise later on in life when people come to us and tell us how grateful they are for what we have helped them achieve. We might coach them on their business operations and life choices or, as was my case, on developing their skills so they can help others even more.

As a chiropractor with twenty years of experience, I have had the privilege of working with and helping people change their lives. It has been an incredible experience. I love being a chiropractor, however, I faced some frustrations when I wanted to make a bigger splash than I could achieve by only seeing clients myself. If you are in business, you will know exactly what this feels like. You know you could be doing so much more, but you need to figure out where to start. You know that you could offer your products or services to many more people if you had the right resources, but it isn't possible because you are stuck, unaware of the next step. For me, the natural thing to do was to take on associates. This way, we could help far more people in our clinic.

By coaching, mentoring, and teaching other practitioners, I have helped them help more people. As a result, I have been able to help many more people get the life-changing treatment they need to continue living longer, healthier, and more comfortable lives. Coaching is not always something that we see as an opportunity to help others achieve more. We might see it as an experience that only supports one other person – the person we are directly coaching. And yet, as I saw in our business, the coaching had an incredible ripple effect. My associates weren't the only ones to benefit from the coaching. Of course, they benefited from growing their skills and expanding their knowledge but beyond this, the treatments they could provide their patients with were also the remarkable results of this coaching.

Coaching can change lives. Patients who would previously have needed to wait weeks to see me could finally see a practitioner within just a few days, making sure that they could function better much faster than before. Of course, this ripple effect affected me as a business owner as well, and I saw my business get a real boost.

This chapter is the story of my experience as a coach. Unfortunately, my coaching experience wasn't always sunshine and rainbows – like most people in the world, I also experienced times when I doubted myself but, I overcame it, and this is how.

MY ENTRY INTO THE COACHING WORLD

When I first graduated from university, the most important transaction I was looking for in my first job was not simply financial security but also knowledge, and finding a clinic that valued coaching and mentoring was my priority. This was difficult as not all places do so, but I was determined. Working in the right environment should allow you to grow and become a better version of yourself. We spend a significant proportion of our lives at work, an incredible amount of time on the scale of a lifetime and it would be a shame to be doing something that does not allow us to grow, something that we do not feel we can learn from.

Coaching and mentoring are essential for any business to grow and thrive, regardless of the service you offer or the products you sell. We all want a team of people who take pride in their work and are not just there to go through the motions to pick up a paycheque. Attracting and keeping the right people means that we need to invest in them. We need to invest in their personal and professional development. We want our businesses to grow. We all want to continue developing and becoming better versions of ourselves, and this is where coaching and mentoring come in – one person teaches the other how to improve something, become better, or make the most of opportunities. This is how we grow as people and avoid this stagnation.

As I graduated from university and entered the clinical world, having access to a coach and mentor was incredibly helpful. It effectively helped bridge the gap from university to clinical life, which can be quite a jump, after all, university involves studying, writing essays, and doing practical exams. Although I spent the last year in Uni in the in-house clinic seeing "real patients", this was under the close supervision of our clinical tutors. Applying what you learned in a clinical setting where all the decisions are resting in your own hands is different. You are dealing with real lives, people who have real pain and aches and are coming to you for help, so, you can feel a lot of pressure to help them reach their goals.

I also knew that I was putting a lot on my own shoulders. I had high expectations for myself. I wanted to ensure that I was doing my best for my patients, fulfilling the clinic's expectations, representing them well, and not letting myself down. Having put so much effort into getting my qualifications, I naturally wanted to make the most out of my education and showcase my skills. That turned out to be quite a sticking point for me. Letting others down is one thing – you can come up with reasons. For example, you can say that you haven't learned certain skills or don't know enough about something yet to contribute, but when you don't live up to your own standards, no excuse can make you feel good about yourself. As you may know yourself, living up to your own expectations can sometimes be your biggest challenge… it was certainly mine.

This is why I sought a clinic where I knew I would get good mentoring. Living up to these expectations can feel overwhelming when you do not know where to start, but thankfully, there was someone there to help me figure it out. I had a coach from the outset, someone. who in the early days mainly acted as a mentor. They would help me tone down the expectations and remind me that I was just at the beginning of my career or that it was all very well that I wanted to do everything perfectly, but this simply wasn't possible without experience, so I should be more forgiving of myself., I can't stress how important my first experience with a coach was– they showed me that while expectations were great to push ourselves to do better, they also can hold us back from experimenting with other avenues if we become too stubborn and focused on what we want to achieve, instead of focusing on what else there is to explore.

But it goes beyond that. When I first started, I dealt with all kinds of self-doubt. I wasn't confident of what I was doing a lot of the time. I was new to the field and was doing my best, but I did not always feel I was getting it right. These self-doubts were there every step of the way. I often felt like I wasn't sure what I was doing, whether I was doing the right thing or doing it correctly. As a chiropractor, making a mistake could have significant repercussions, so I was glad to have a coach there to help me figure things out. My coach was equally there to make me more confident about my decision-making and to encourage me when I doubted myself.

Now, there's a different part of the puzzle that I also struggled with – imposter syndrome. Unfortunately, this is something I had to deal with quite a bit. Most of us struggle with it to some extent, especially in the medical field since you are working with people's bodies and a mistake can have significant consequences. You might feel like you aren't qualified enough, can't do your job as well as the others can, or aren't as talented as the others. You might also worry that others will see this and call you out, even though you are fully qualified. This is where, again, a coach came in to help me. I was dealing with all shades of imposter syndrome – feeling as though I wasn't good enough to be working with patients yet like others were better than me… the list goes on but yet again, mentorship and coaching came in handy. I had someone there to tell me when I was being unreasonable, and I had people there to push me when necessary. Coaching and mentoring can do this – it helps you get past the hurdles when you aren't sure what to do, don't know what to do next, and aren't sure of yourself.

Teaching and mentoring aren't the same thing. Teaching is something that a person in a school, for example, can do. With a teacher, you learn something specific. For example, you might learn how different body parts work in certain ways. You might learn anatomy, physiology, neurology, how people's minds work with their bodies, and how they are interconnected - for example, a patient might not be at their best because their body is misaligned, or that it might also be associated with other aspects of their life (e.g., chronic stress, relationship problems, work, habits, nutrition, exercise or the lack thereof, and so on). Although you can learn these things from reading or attending seminars, nothing beats experience. Being able to draw on somebody else's experience can be extremely useful.

While a teacher is mainly responsible for imparting knowledge or skills in a specific subject area, mainly within a formal educational setting such as a school or a university, a mentor mostly gives you guidance, advice, and support based on their experience, knowledge, and expertise. Their approach is usually personalised and tailored to your needs, aspirations, and circumstances. So, mentors, typically, do not follow a structured curriculum or programme like a teacher.

What I had was a mentor. It was someone who saw me, a recent graduate who was entirely new to the field and decided to help me become the best version of myself. My mentor saw my potential and that I could achieve great things, but I needed that extra push. My experience with my initial mentors and the coaches and teachers I was fortunate to learn from later inspired me to be a mentor and coach myself.

My early coaching experience was mainly with a mentor. I learned through their experience and guidance. As I evolved and my circumstances changed, I required different knowledge and skills. As a result, I have worked with many mentors and coaches throughout my career, and this is something I continue to do. I have learned so much from these amazing people, and they have helped shape me as a chiropractor, business owner, mentor, and coach.

WHAT CAME NEXT?

Fast-forward to many years later and it was my turn to be a mentor, coach, and teacher. I wanted others to benefit from the skills and knowledge I had gained through the years and wanted to help them to be able to help more people. I had accumulated a lot of knowledge and experience accumulated from running a business with a team for over ten years. I had trained them, done team building days, supported them, mentored them, and coached them. Speaking to other business owners from other sectors made me realise that most of what we did in the clinic was applicable across most businesses.

In fact, when buying the clinic, we took it from where it was with a team of eight to a team of nineteen at one point, before we sold the practice. It was a steep learning curve. We had not been taught anything about business at university, so we had to learn everything from scratch - running a team, creating systems, hiring, firing, finances, overheads and marketing to list just a few things. We spent a lot of time and resources attending seminars and finding the right coaches and mentors who could help us refine our vision for the business and the knowledge to make it a reality.

Getting this all in place meant I could reduce my hours to spend more time running the business, coaching, and mentoring the team. This way, the clinic was helping far more people than we could have done before we expanded the team. We eventually sold the business to our practice manager and one of the associate chiropractors, which meant that there was the perfect handover in terms of continuation, both for the team and the patients. I am still practising as a chiropractor but also focusing on the coaching and mentoring part of my business.

I have always loved doing extensive continued learning and development in my chiropractic career. It has ensured continued improvements and has kept my work exciting and progressive. It was only natural for me to apply this to my coaching as well. This training opened my eyes to pure coaching. I had already been exposed to many techniques, tools, and approaches throughout my career, however, this approach appealed to me. The most exciting part was the angle of coaching the person rather than coaching their situation or adding to their knowledge. It can be applied whether I am familiar with the kind of business or job they do or not. Adding this skill to my repertoire has allowed me to coach people I would not have been able to help previously.

Nowadays, my main passion lies in coaching business owners, especially the owners of small-to-medium-sized businesses, who are going through some of the challenges I did myself in the time I built and ran what was, at the time, one of the top chiropractic clinics in the UK.

We divided our team coaching into a few key themes to ensure a solid structure. We also needed to cover all the areas required to cater to a diverse team with different requirements. The sessions could be on key performance indicators, clinical skills for the clinicians, customer care, philosophy, case studies, techniques/systems, as well as personalised coaching on an ongoing basis, asking questions such as: How could you ensure the best performance possible? How could we help as many people and patients as effectively as possible, and what did this mean in terms of the key performance indicators we needed to hit? Did we have the systems in place to ensure that we could help more people without losing the personal touch? Did we need to respond to their emails more quickly? Did we need to get new systems in place to reduce the number of phone calls we received to allow us to improve customer care for the patients whilst they were attending the clinic? This also meant that, as an owner, I had to learn how to take on feedback. If a patient left negative feedback, I had to take it constructively. I had to use it to improve our offering and I had to take on this feedback constructively, even if customers could share it with us in a rather hurtful way. I had to change how the team reacted in these moments – how was this information helpful to us as a clinic, and how could we use it to improve our standards and provide better services?

One of the things I love about coaching is that there is no "right" way of doing it. This allows you to put your own DNA on what you do. You can be a mentor, a consultant where you teach, and a coach who partners with your clients and allows them to find their way without you adding your own opinions. You can also combine the above. I allow for a combination of these depending on who I am coaching and their needs and wants. After all, the goal is to enable them to gain the clarity to achieve their objectives that align with their values and vision.

I wouldn't have become the chiropractor, mentor, and coach I am today if it hadn't been for all the fantastic and knowledgeable people I have had the privilege to work with throughout my career. They provided knowledge, certainty, and clarity, and at the same time, they gave me the autonomy to grow. This allowed me to assimilate their input and expertise to make me a better practitioner, mentor, and coach in my way.

It can be challenging to see someone doing something in a way that you don't entirely agree with and still letting them do it, however, when coaching associates, I had to work with them to find what was congruent with their beliefs and personalities to maximise their interaction with their patients. That meant that it wasn't necessarily how I would do it or how I would say something. I had to get on board with that because, at the end of the day, the important thing was that the patients got the best possible outcome.

The more they learned about the kinds of KPIs they needed to hit, and how to look out for them and understand why it was necessary to meet them, the more they became autonomous. The result? Happier associates, happier patients, and even happier business owners. I would say that one of the most satisfying things about mentoring practitioners was to see them go on to open up their own successful practices and take on their own associates who could help them grow and help more and more people. Talk about the ripple effect!

THE RIPPLE EFFECT: CHANGES FOR THE BETTER

How did this improve our sphere of influence, you wonder? Ultimately, our goal was always to help patients access better care and more efficiently. Accessing healthcare support can be challenging. People often don't know what they want, just that they don't want to be in pain anymore. Speaking to them, understanding what is important to them and using this information to help them reach their goals can be incredibly rewarding. Most of the time, we could do this by treating them in our clinic, but it could involve helping them find a different approach that aligned more with what they wanted to achieve. While some people go to their chiropractor for regular adjustments, often, patients only come to us as a last resort or when they are in pain again; when they've tried everything else, unsuccessfully, and finally come to us to see if we can help them. These people would come to us when they were suffering, when they'd been in pain for days, weeks, or even longer, and they were almost out of hope. We needed to give them a solution and some hope that their bodies could regulate, repair, and heal themselves and that they would finally be able to live without this chronic pain. This means providing excellent customer service, which starts with high quality and prompt service. By coaching the team, teaching them about systems, showing them how to best deal with situations, and encouraging them to develop themselves and take charge, we made it possible for thousands of clients to be taken in and treated as soon as possible. We increased our clinic's capacity by hiring and coaching the right people, making it easier for patients to get help promptly without waiting too long to see a professional.

Doing this also made it possible for the clinic to become more credible, to be seen as a leader in its field, and to become the place for chiropractic care in our area. The more people had access to the clinic's services, the more recommendations we had, and the cycle kept repeating. The goal was always to help as many people as possible, which was only possible if we touched enough people's lives. One of the most important lessons I learned while coaching my team was to make others qualified and skilled enough to do what I was doing without needing to be there in person. Likewise, as a coach, my role is not to tell my clients how to do something but to coach them to find the solution that works for them. Approaching coaching from this angle creates autonomy, and the results are far better and more sustainable this way. In our clinic, this was the real ripple effect; the people we coached gained excellent skills and our clinic benefitted from their increased experience which, in turn, they could take with them to other jobs in the future. Of course, the ultimate ripple effect was felt by the patients who benefitted greatly from the improved support and treatments our amazing team could provide them.

Looking back, I could only coach others this way because of the experience I had gained through those I had worked with. My experience of being coached and mentored profoundly impacted me because I knew what worked well for me and what did not. It shaped what sort of coach and mentor I wanted to be.

UP NEXT: WHAT TO EXPECT

My coaching career may have started with me being mentored and coached as a newly-graduated chiropractor. It began with clinical skills and knowledge and then expanded into personal development, customer service, business skills and learning to run a team. When reading this chapter, you may not have imagined that chiropractic was a world where mentoring or coaching would be so widespread and important, but it is highly prevalent and widely accepted. I have also found that the skills required within a chiropractic business are highly transferable. Whether this is problem-solving, running mixed teams, customer service or excellent communication skills, they are all important in most other companies and sectors.

I believe coaching is something that will become more and more accepted and popular. I have experienced mentoring and coaching first-hand and seen its profound effects on me as a practitioner, business owner and person. As more people understand that they can benefit from coaching, they will become more and more curious, therefore, we, as coaches, must ensure we are well-equipped to meet them where they are — helping people understand what coaching is and that it doesn't mean they need to be perfect. Success doesn't mean doing what the coach is doing but finding something that works for them and their situation. I also think it is fascinating, as we can use our backgrounds to help people in our unique ways. For example, my strength is to coach the owners of small-to-medium-sized businesses, not just with their business needs but with the balance of their business and health needs. My background as a chiropractor means that I have many skills that can help people make better decisions, not just for their business but also for their health and relationships, which will significantly impact their business and personal lives. One of my favourite sayings is, "True healthcare is self-care." Finding this balance as a busy business owner can be incredibly challenging, yet making the right decisions regarding your health will profoundly impact your business. Over the years, I have seen way too many successful business owners have significant regrets over letting other parts of their lives suffer in their pursuit of "success". Getting this balance right can be incredibly rewarding.

Coaching has brought me a lot personally. Having mentors and coaches over the years to keep pushing me forward, to hold me accountable, to hold my hand and be there for me when I was struggling is something I will be forever grateful for.

Unfortunately, too many young people who enter their fields leave or quit because they doubt themselves, feel like they don't belong or don't have what it takes to make the impact they want. Too many aspiring business owners give up or burn out because they don't have the support they need. Too many successful business owners struggle with balancing their work and personal life and, as a result, see their health or relationships decline. What if we could solve these problems with high-quality coaching and mentoring?

Likewise, I want to continue helping businesses thrive. I help business owners get a clear vision of their company and business, and I help them get the framework and systems needed in place. I want to continue helping them organise their business, so they know where and how to grow it.

I love helping other healthcare practitioners to help more people, but I wanted to increase the ripple effects even further. The best way of doing this is to coach business owners. I know the stresses and challenges of running a business, having a team, and feeling very isolated without anyone to lean on when making big decisions. Being able to coach people through these challenging periods is something I'm passionate about. People must know how to find the right work-life balance. This might mean organising the business better, sustainably growing the business, or learning how to balance family, hobbies, travel, and so on. The bottom line is that coaching is about helping individuals create their future in their unique vision.

WHAT'S THE TAKEAWAY?

With business coaching, we want to help the individual business - and its people - improve and grow., whether through better processes and organisation, identifying where they can enhance skills and client interaction or increasing referrals. The result? Better client outcomes and higher satisfaction, and hence, enhanced industry reputation. Likewise, coaching can lead to improved business management and increased growth. Coaching can also be an investment in the team, where the business owner can outsource the coaching and mentoring of their team to allow them to focus their time and energy on other aspects of their business. Many of my clients, whether they are lawyers, healthcare professionals or entrepreneurs, run their own practices and businesses but they still might need help taking the business to the next level or help finding the balance between business and personal life.

As we journey through the world of business coaching, we can circle back to the profound words of B.J. Palmer, "We never know how far-reaching something we may think, say or do today will affect the lives of millions tomorrow." This sentiment echoes powerfully through every aspect of coaching. The ripple effects can be immense and far-reaching, whether coaching a fledgling entrepreneur, a seasoned business owner, or a health-care practitioner. Each small change, each piece of advice, and each moment of guidance can set off a chain reaction that extends well beyond the immediate coaching relationship.

Coaching is not just about addressing the present; it's about shaping the future. It's about empowering individuals to make impactful decisions, not just for their businesses, but for them-selves, the communities they serve and the lives they touch. In doing so, coaches catalyse a ripple effect of positive change, growth, and development that reverberates through time and space. The effects of our coaching today may not be fully realised immediately, but like ripples in a pond, they spread outwards, touching lives and influencing futures in ways we can scarcely imagine.

As coaches, we hold a responsibility and a privilege. We have the power to initiate change, to inspire action, and to guide towards a brighter, more prosperous future. In embracing this role, we honour the essence of B.J. Palmer's words and contribute to a legacy that extends well beyond our direct reach, affecting the lives of millions tomorrow through the actions we take and the guidance we provide today.

ABOUT MORTEN ISNES

Morten is a Business and Wellness coach. He is passionate about helping business owners who are stressed, overwhelmed, time-poor and sometimes struggle with their own health by helping them implement business and lifestyle strategies.

Since obtaining his chiropractic degree in 2003, Morten has worked in a private clinical setting, enabling thousands of people to achieve their health goals through a combination of hands-on care and helping them improve their lifestyles. As a mentor and coach, he has worked with clinicians, entrepreneurs, business owners, and managers, many of whom faced challenges in maintaining their health amidst the demands of their businesses.

Drawing on his extensive experience working in clinics, and growing and managing his own successful clinic over the past two decades, Morten brings a wealth of practical knowledge and empathetic understanding to his coaching. His approach is deeply influenced by his own journey. As an introvert in a bustling business environment, he had to learn the importance of finding equilibrium between interactive, high-energy, professional roles and the need for personal quiet time and reflection. His holistic approach helps to create a healthy business from the inside, which is sustainable in the long term.

Outside his coaching practice, Morten cherishes the outdoors as a sanctuary for relaxation and rejuvenation. He finds solace and inspiration in nature, whether it's through tranquil walks, playing golf, or riding his motorbike. His love for the outdoors reflects his quest for balance and is integral to his life philosophy, influencing his unique approach to coaching and personal well-being.

You can reach Morten at **https://linktr.ee/mortenisnes** or simply scan the QR Code below:

11

WEAVING A GOLDEN THREAD OF PLAY — TAMZIN HALL

ADDING A PLAYFUL APPROACH TO COACHING

Join me, Tamzin, on a transformative journey as I introduce the enchanting world of play in coaching. This chapter reveals my personal evolution which began by infusing play into my coaching approach.

In this chapter, we will explore the profound benefits of playfulness. Through captivating real-life tales, we will investigate how play can spark joy and authenticity both in coaching and in life. Please be reassured, that all names have changed to protect my client's identity.

Let's start by sharing the tangible impact I've had on my clients.

When Kylie first came to our initial coaching session, she was carrying a heavy burden of frustration and felt trapped in the never-ending cycle of monotony. Although she wasn't experiencing depression, her feeling of being stuck was undeniable.

We've all faced situations that made every workday feel like an uphill battle.

As we embarked on our coaching journey, we introduced a touch of playfulness to her daily routine. For instance, I encouraged her to ask herself, "If you were a superhero, what would you do now?" This simple question breathed new life into her perspective, infusing creativity and enthusiasm into her approach to everyday challenges. With this playful mindset, Kylie broke free from the chains of stagnation and went on to thrive in a successful and fulfilling career.

As we know, coaching is a powerful vehicle for personal transformation, for helping individuals unshackle themselves from the quagmire of life's challenges, and that's precisely why I ventured into this field. I want to empower people to move forward and find enjoyment in the journey. It's not just about breaking free from the rut; it's about infusing joy, creativity, and a sense of play into both professional and personal lives. That's where the real magic happens.

By introducing a playful space for my clients to explore their own ideas of fun and play, not just in their leisure time, but also in their work environments, together, we open the door to a world of transformation. For me, coaching is about helping them see their circumstances through the lens of curiosity, akin to the questions a child might ask or the imaginative leaps a superhero might take. It's about embracing a different perspective, reframing challenges, and letting playfulness illuminate their path. It's not just about professional success; it's about creating a life that's fulfilling, enjoyable, and fundamentally fun. Fun doesn't diminish professionalism; it enhances it, making our interactions more meaningful, our teams more cohesive, and our work environments more conducive to growth.

Of course, there are moments when the gravity of life's challenges cannot be sugar-coated. Some clients come to me with heavy hearts, burdened by grief or navigating through painful situations. In those instances, the introduction of play is more subtle. It is not always labelled as "play," but it's there, guiding them towards healing and growth.

My client, Peter, faced high conflict and tension in his professional environment. Traditional thinking no longer sufficed, so we explored the options and decided to introduce LEGO as a creative tool for collaborative problem-solving. With LEGO, meetings became engaging and lighter. The team used LEGO models to express ideas and create shared visions. The question, "What does your LEGO model look like if your team achieves its goals?" unlocked new possibilities. Over time, this approach dissolved tension and fostered camaraderie and creativity. Peter's leadership evolved, and the organisation benefitted from his fresh, unconventional thinking. LEGO had initiated a ripple of positive change.

This ripple effect engenders happiness, joy, and a host of other positive outcomes. It's the catalyst for enhanced performance, the cultivation of the right organisational culture, improved team morale, and effective conflict management. It reduces anxiety and stress, and ushers in a sea of positivity. All this is achieved simply by being a bit more playful, a bit more imaginative, and a bit more daring.

Let's take a journey back to 2001. I was sitting in my manager's office after a particularly challenging conversation with one of my team members. His question, "How did that make you feel?" left me stumped. As the meeting continued, he skilfully guided me through understanding the situation from another perspective, and without realising it, I was introduced to the power of coaching. The face of this transformative experience was Mr. Anderson, a manager like no other. I can recall the office we were sitting in as if it was yesterday. It had tall ceilings, dark blue carpeting, and a large desk, behind which sat Mr Anderson. The man himself bore a comforting resemblance to Father Christmas, all twinkling eyes and a demeanour that was compassionate, never stern, or cross. That meeting changed my life. Mr. Anderson instilled in me the belief that anything was possible, and I left the office that day with the realisation that everything was about to change. The prospect of change excited me, as I always thrive on the anticipation of what lies ahead.

Several years down the line, my life had undergone significant transformation. I had the personal life I had always dreamed of but professionally, I still felt trapped. The memory of Mr. Anderson was fading, and the life I envisioned during our conversations seemed like a distant dream. I had grown and achieved remarkable success in both my personal and professional life, but there was an underlying feeling that something was amiss. It was in the midst of this uncertainty that I had a moment of clarity. I was on my way to a physiotherapy appointment, following multiple back surgeries and I was frequently in intense pain. I arrived at the appointment and a happy dog with a wagging tail stopped me in my tracks. The thought that entered my head was, "What do I need to feel as happy as that dog?" It dawned on me that I did not feel that I was accomplishing what I aspired to. This realisation lingered as I entered the physiotherapist's room. Looking back, I felt similar to how Kylie felt when we first met.

I lay on the blue bed in the partitioned room with my head resting on a disposable paper pillow. Jenny, the physiotherapist, asked, "How are you, Tamzin?" and it felt like a bottle had been uncorked. I shared with Jenny how stuck I felt, how much I loathed my job and the intense inner conflict I experienced. I yearned to achieve the goals Mr. Anderson had believed I could attain, but I felt hindered. It was Jenny's turn to have an impact, just as Mr. Anderson had. She posed a question that would resonate for years: "Tamzin if you could do anything, what would you do? Who would you be?" She left me with that question until our next session. Jenny's coaching approach mirrored Mr. Anderson's, and I knew I needed something more, something greater. These two individuals had shown me that I could achieve more, though it didn't happen overnight.

Almost a decade has passed since my final session with Jenny. Today, I find myself fulfilled, content, and making a substantial difference. The journey was far from easy, but it was undoubtedly worth it. I left Jenny's cubicle and decided my future included completing something I had always dreamed of - a degree in psychology, and yes, I achieved this whilst working full-time. Hard work became my constant companion. As a person with dyslexia, I was told I'd never earn a degree. It took four years of balancing my full-time job, family responsibilities, and late-night and early-morning study sessions to prove them wrong. But, with the support of my husband, son, and my parents., I did prove them wrong, and graduating was one of the proudest moments of my life.

Following my graduation, I embarked on a coaching course, driven by the desire to help people as Mr Anderson and Jenny had helped me. I wanted to make a more significant impact and combine my experiences, qualifications, and knowledge to coach in a controlled and professional manner. Initially, I aspired to be a leadership coach due to my corporate background and newly acquired degree, but I soon discovered that the traditional corporate blueprint, with its one-size-fits-all approach, was unsustainable – for me, anyway. I yearned for excitement, enjoyment, and a way to escape the corporate coaching trap that I was inadvertently sliding into. Generally speaking, corporate life treated me well. I found some satisfaction in my roles, particularly in my accomplishments, however, a colleague once posed a thought-provoking question: "Do you ever feel like a small cog in the vast corporate machinery, constantly churning, concurring, and doing, without instigating change?" This question continues to resonate with me today, and it fuels my desire for transformation. No one should experience this sentiment, and if your organisation fosters such an environment, it's time for a shift. It is time for them to embrace the future, move away from archaic processes and procedures and open their staff and their business to everything possible. This, my friends, is my mission: to provide everyone with the opportunity to be the catalyst for change, to effect change, and to thrive - with the right support and belief, anything is possible - as Mr. Anderson demonstrated to me.

One day, while coaching Jo, a remarkable individual, I witnessed a powerful realisation. She had climbed the corporate ladder, relentlessly worked long hours, smashed target after target, and ascended to a director-level position, yet she found her job uninspiring and felt engulfed in corporate red tape. I posed a question to Jo, inspired by Jenny's earlier question to me: "If your role could be anything you want it to be, what would it be?" Jo's response was profound; she expressed a desire for a role similar to a character from a television show. Katie, AKA Killer Frost from The Flash - although with less of the killer and more focus on the white hair and dark clothes!

We embarked on a journey filled with playful exploration. There is always another way, a unique path to follow.

The excitement was palpable when Jo returned the following week. She had transformed her office into a space that reflected her personality, just like Killer Frost, embracing play and uniqueness. The idea may have seemed unconventional, and many corporate organisations discourage such self-expression, but through my work with neurodivergent individuals, I have come to understand their need for a personal, safe, and stimulating office space. Jo's journey into embracing her distinctiveness and play ignited my own. Simultaneously working on my dissertation about bringing play into the workplace, I decided to attend a webinar on play – not necessarily centred around playful coaching but exploring the broader concept of play and the magic that unfolds when we open our minds to new possibilities.

A year later, my journey of infusing a playful approach into my coaching practice unveiled a realm of boundless opportunities. I had achieved full qualification, obtained my ACC (Associate Certified Coach), and was now firmly set on the path toward PCC (Professional Certified Coach), and I had graduated from university.

This transition from where I was all those years ago, sitting with Mr Anderson and talking to Jenny, was nothing short of a game-changer. When I talk about a playful approach, I'm not referring to the idea of introducing a box of toys into every coaching session, although I must admit that incorporating Lego into boardroom discussions can be a tremendously enjoyable and transformative experience. My intention isn't to propose team-building exercises either. My purpose is to help people achieve the feeling I felt on my graduation day, dancing in the rain, marching across the graduation stage beaming, skipping down the road, and watching a sunset with the people you love. My purpose is to guide people to look for those pockets of fun and play every day. That's the magic.

Marco was brimming with enthusiasm after our coaching session, he was determined to find a way to unite his team outside of their workplace, fostering camaraderie and a deeper sense of personal connection. He set out to brainstorm ideas that would resonate with his team's preferences. Bursting into the room during our next meeting, he excitedly declared his grand plan. "I have it! I've got the perfect idea!" Curious, I inquired about his brainchild. He planned to rent a gliding facility for a day and take his entire team gliding…

You are likely thinking that such an adventure could either be a dream come true or a nightmare. That's the essence of the matter when it comes to play – it must align with the inclinations and interests of all participants. Playful activities, if undertaken as a group, must be carefully orchestrated to ensure that they foster enjoyment rather than anxiety. It's been my observation that team-building exercises, in particular, tend to fall short of pleasing everyone, unless they are meticulously thought through. In the case of my client's grandiose gliding scheme, it is easy to imagine the ensuing chaos. Approximately half the team would flatly refuse, while the other half would spend sleepless nights racked with severe anxiety.

This shift towards a playful approach in my coaching practice was largely inspired by a remarkable online seminar I attended, which delved into how adults could incorporate elements of play into their daily lives. The insights gleaned from this experience, combined with my coaching training and my dissertation on how play contributes to workplace happiness, led me to adopt a more playful disposition in my coaching interactions. While there are instances where playful approaches may not be suitable, such as when coaching individuals grappling with grief, tragedy, or trauma, the essence of play extends beyond games or toys. It entails adopting a mindset that seeks unique perspectives, different angles, and creative solutions.

This transformation in my approach, especially when working with neurodivergent individuals, has been rather remarkable. It seems that the neurodivergent brain has an affinity for play, appreciating the opportunity to explore alternative pathways. To my delight, this alignment between play and the neurodivergent mind has led to some extraordinary breakthroughs in our coaching sessions. Imagine it as lying on your back on a sunny day, gazing at the clouds and transforming them into various objects or finding shapes in the foam of your coffee cup.

Fostering a playful perspective is something I now implicitly encourage my clients to do, sometimes without explicitly labelling it as such. While I may not be particularly fond of labels, the essence of this approach is to open our eyes to the possibilities of fun, injecting a sense of joy into a world that often feels rigid, monochrome, and exasperating. It's like adding a splash of colour to an otherwise stark and colourless environment.

Whether it is introducing a fidget toy or some coloured pens onto your desk, embarking on a walk in the woods, playing with your dog, swinging on swings, splashing in puddles, or engaging in any other playful endeavour, the aim is to infuse your day with that extra dose of excitement. This infusion of play can have a remarkable impact on your well-being, creativity, and overall happiness. Activities that evoke play foster a sense of joy, reduce stress, and enhance problem-solving skills.

It's about embracing play in whatever form resonates with you, which ultimately leads to a more enriched and fulfilling life.

The beauty of a playful approach lies not in the specific activities themselves, but rather in the feelings they evoke. Research, studies, and my own experiences have all pointed to the same conclusion – it's not about the activity per se, but rather about how it makes us feel. This is especially relevant when working with teams and groups. The emphasis should be on creating feelings of connection, a sense of belonging, and the belief that every individual plays a pivotal role in contributing to a greater whole. That's where the true magic lies.

In the end, it doesn't matter whether your chosen approach is playful, musical, communicative, sustainable, or environmental. What matters is that it's uniquely yours. If you could customise and personalise your approach, what would it look like? What if you could craft a coaching, communication, or leadership approach that knows no bounds? The implementation need not be immediate – after all, my conversation with Mr. Anderson took place over two decades ago, and I'm still evolving and still fine-tuning my approach to incorporate playfulness. I have a profound appreciation for laughter, and I believe that humour can elevate virtually any situation. Play, similarly, has the potential to transform our experiences.

Adding a playful approach to your life, coaching practice, and everything you do is all about believing in your unique style. It's about breaking free from the limitations you impose on yourself and embracing the idea that it's never too late to infuse playfulness into your journey. I've often wondered if I could have started this journey of playful coaching sooner, but regrets won't lead us to where we want to be. When I doubt this, I have only to look at my son (a budding golfer) and his perspective on his game.

"If I hadn't made that bad shot, I wouldn't have had the game I did. If I hadn't hit the ball that way at that time, I wouldn't have achieved what I did." The wisdom in this statement is undeniable. Life, like golf, is full of swings—some better than others. And just as each swing contributes to your golf game, every experience shapes you into the person you are today. We mustn't dwell on what could have been done differently; instead, we should focus on creating the life we genuinely enjoy and move forward.

Incorporating a playful approach into every aspect of your life is a choice that lies entirely in your hands. Your life is your canvas, and you have the creative power to paint it with colours of playfulness, fun, excitement, joy, and fulfilment. It's essential to ensure that you're painting it for yourself with the colours you chose and not to meet someone else's expectations. If you're living your life to please others or adhering to a corporate, black-and-white script because you think it's what's expected of you, then it is time for a change.

Your inner reluctance, your resistance to change, and your apprehension about how others may judge your choices are the only obstacles that stand between you and the playful, fulfilling, life you desire. These obstacles are like self-imposed limitations, but breaking free from them is within your reach.

Consider the world of superheroes. Think about Spider-Man. If Peter Parker had let Tony Stark's opinions guide his actions, he would never have become Spider-Man. Tony believed Peter was too young and if Peter had listened, he wouldn't have swung from skyscrapers or made the profound impact he did. So, take a page from the superhero playbook, and be uniquely you. Embrace playfulness, infuse fun into your life, and paint it with your colours, because playfulness is different for each of us.

In the end, there's no single formula or blueprint for incorporating a playful approach. It's a personal journey. And yes, it can be daunting to step outside the comfort zone, challenge the expectations, and embrace a more playful and colourful life. But remember, the only real obstacle is the belief that it can't be done.

I am not waiting for a better time. I infuse playfulness into my life, my coaching practice, and all that I do NOW. I am diving headfirst into my unique style because the opportunity to create a world full of play, fun, and excitement is right here, right now, and I am encouraging my clients and those in my world to do the same.

As I've navigated the path to creating a coaching practice that is uniquely mine, I've been privileged to work with remarkable leaders from various organisations. What's become evident in my journey is the transformative power of opening my clients' eyes to the realm of possibilities. It's not just about individual growth; it's about creating a ripple effect that extends beyond my immediate sphere.

In many cases, my clients are at the helm of organisations, and their leadership and decision-making directly impact the teams they lead. When I assist these leaders in broadening their horizons and thinking expansively through the power of play, the impact extends far beyond the coaching sessions. They, in turn, inspire their teams to adopt a similar mindset, encouraging them to envision bigger and more ambitious goals.

One recent client's story encapsulates this ripple effect beautifully. This client was embroiled in a challenging situation where they needed to collaborate with another team on a project. The collaboration was fraught with conflict, primarily due to clashing personalities, assertive egos, strong opinions, and extensive experience, along with deeply ingrained beliefs that each team's approach was the definitive path to success. Meeting after meeting was marked by tension and disputes, and the project was at a standstill. Valuable hours were spent locked in a boardroom, with the prevailing sentiment being that they were not just stagnant but regressing. The project's deadline was ominously close, and the client was paying a significant cost for an endeavour that appeared to be moving backwards due to the overpowering egos in the room.

Now, it is worth noting that having diverse personalities in a team is essential. We need varied perspectives to stimulate creativity and problem-solving. However, when these differing personalities result in incessant shouting and a cacophony of voices vying for dominance, the waters become muddied, and progress stalls.

At this critical juncture, we embarked on a journey to explore a different approach and what it could look like. I posed a question to my client that was somewhat unconventional. I asked, "What if, in the next meeting, everyone around the table showed up dressed as an animal? What animal would each of them be?" The responses were as diverse as the personalities in the room. We had tigers, lions, gorillas, and even a kitten.

Now, the real question was, how could the quieter, more reserved individuals be heard amid the roar of the lions and the ferociousness of the gorillas? The answer was surprisingly insightful. The gorilla needed to be preoccupied with specific tasks, like eating or engaging in certain activities, to create space for the kitten's voice to be heard. When it was the gorilla's turn to share, the kitten reciprocated the favour. An essential aspect was identifying a leader within the group, someone who could manage the dynamics. In my client's view, they were the lion, but they also realised they had been contributing to the chaos with their own strong-willed ego.

Did my client share the details of this animal metaphor with their colleagues in the boardroom? Probably not. But that's the beauty of coaching. In a safe and supportive environment, we can experiment with unconventional ideas, explore novel perspectives, and think beyond the constraints of convention. This playful approach allowed us to re-imagine the situation, finding a way to foster productive collaboration in a group teeming with diverse personalities.

When my client subsequently entered the boardroom, they carried with them sacks of fidget toys, coloured pens, paper, flip charts, snacks galore and refreshments. They divided the group into smaller teams, each comprising a unique combination of animal personalities. For instance, a kitten worked alongside a giraffe, each playing their part. The kitten, the 'soft and cute' leader, adeptly managed the project, knowing when to employ its 'claws' to assert its authority.

By infusing this playful element into the proceedings, the team not only completed the project on time but exceeded everyone's expectations. The group worked collaboratively and harmoniously, highlighting the incredible potential for different personality types to come together and excel. The result was a resounding success that earned the team an esteemed award within the company.

This is the essence of the ripple effect. It's the idea that a single transformation within an individual - in this case, my client - can set in motion a series of positive changes that radiate outward, touching the lives and experiences of many others. The effect isn't limited to the immediate situation; it extends to the team, the organisation, and even beyond, leaving an indelible mark.

The success of one team, inspired by a fresh approach, can inspire other teams and departments to explore new ways of working. This newfound openness to creativity and collaboration becomes a part of the organisation's culture, redefining how they tackle challenges, innovate, and operate as a collective.

As more and more individuals and teams within the organisation experience these positive shifts, the impact continues to widen and deepen. It's not just about the initial project; it's about fostering a transformative culture that promotes innovation and collaboration at every level. The power of play influences not only the company's operations but also its relationships with clients, partners, and the broader industry.

In my role as a coach, this ripple effect has become a touchstone of my practice. I'm not just guiding individuals; I'm fostering a broader transformation. I'm empowering my clients to make waves, to challenge the status quo, and to inspire change that transcends their immediate circumstances. The power of coaching, when coupled with a playful and creative mindset, is that it doesn't just impact one person or one team; it has the capacity to influence entire organisations, industries, and communities. It is a beautiful reminder that when we choose to explore the bounds of possibility, we're not just altering our own lives. We're reshaping the world around us, one ripple at a time.

As I look back on the past twenty-five years of my career, I can't help but marvel at my journey. My mission has evolved, my focus has shifted, and yet, a singular thread has consistently run through my work - my unwavering commitment to supporting others in their growth and achievement. This commitment, this dedication to helping people find their path, is deeply rooted in my core values. Though the journey of fully understanding and bringing these values to life has been a recent exploration, the values themselves—playfulness, grit, zest, authenticity, inclusion, and kindness—have always been part of who I am. These values have guided me through the years. They've been my North Star in times of uncertainty and conflict and have provided me with a sense of direction and purpose. When my actions align with my values, things fall into place.

The exciting thing is that my journey is far from over. In fact, it feels as if I'm standing at the base of a towering mountain, gazing up at countless peaks shrouded in mist. There are an infinite number of dreams to chase, ideas to explore, and summits to reach. The difference now is that I've grown to embrace the process itself. I find joy in every step of the journey, whether it leads to an achievement, a fall, or a moment of self-discovery.

The passage of time naturally brings about evolution. Things that once held great importance may not weigh as heavily on me now. The primary distinction between my mindset today and that of two decades ago is that I'm no longer hesitant to jump into the metaphorical puddle of life. Whether it's with Wellington boots or bare feet, I've learned to embrace the opportunity for fun, even if it means getting a little muddy, a little wet, or even inviting the judgment or laughter of others.

In essence, I've redefined my vision. My goal now is to inspire people to realise the brilliance of their uniqueness and understand that they have the reins to steer their future. If weaving a golden thread of fun and play into their journey is what they desire, then I wholeheartedly encourage it. The world is changing, businesses are evolving, and organisations are growing. The fact that companies like Google, Virgin, and Lego actively encourage their employees to infuse their work with play and innovation is no coincidence. They thrive because they understand the connection between enjoyment and success.

In your job, your business, and your interactions with others, you have the power to be a beacon of light, showing people that work can be enjoyable. I envision two old ladies sitting on a park bench, giggling wholeheartedly. They find amusement in the simplicity of life, whether it is a young man cleaning up after a dog, a child relishing an ice cream, or a dog trying to snatch a lick. The image is a testament to the belief that the best businesses, companies, teams, and individuals are those that relish what they do. When we find joy in our work, we create a ripple effect that attracts others to join in on the fun.

This philosophy transcends personality types. Whether you're an extrovert or an introvert, neurodiverse, neurotypical, or struggling with your mental health. Whether you are a firm believer in having fun through glider rides or watching others on gliders, it is about seeing the world through a playful lens. It is in this state of playfulness that the magic truly unfolds.

So, what comes next on my journey? It is a continuation of sharing this vital message. Organisations and businesses need to embrace their uniqueness. They must do so to attract and retain the best talent. People should walk into work skipping with excitement because they love what they do, not burdened by outdated notions of clocking in and out.

The workplace must be infused with a splash of colour, with countless opportunities and possibilities for the workforce to explore. This is what I aim to convey. I'm determined to help organisations understand that play and fun are not at odds with professionalism. We can take Lego into boardrooms, use visualisation techniques or any other innovative methods as long as our vision is clear. Our vision is what defines success for us and our teams.

In the present climate, it's easy to feel weighed down, constrained, and disheartened, blaming external factors for our struggles. We have a choice. We can either carry the weight of the world on our shoulders or embrace the "Truman Show" mindset. If you haven't seen the film, The Truman Show tells the story of a man who grows up as the unwitting central character in a TV show. Truman knew that the world had more to offer. His mundane routine and his starchy life was not enough. He was ready to break through and be all he knew he was capable of. Similar to Truman, we can escape the mundane, the heavy, and the monotonous.

My vision isn't necessarily that the grass is greener on the other side, or to encourage you to leave your life and sail off to find another, but it is a call to see things differently. Through a playful lens. By approaching life with a playful and joyful mindset, we can find the magic in everything. I envision a world where we never stop believing that we can reach the moon, the stars, or any other dream we dare to imagine.

To ask a group of six-year-olds about their future aspirations is to hear dreams of becoming astronauts or racing drivers, but what happens when we ask the same question to a room of twenty-five-year-olds? We get answers like accountant, solicitor, or funeral director. Somewhere along the way, we lose sight of the boundless potential that play, and a youthful sense of adventure bring. It is time to reclaim that spirit and infuse our lives with a dash of playfulness and fun.

Your unique style, your one-of-a-kind approach can truly change the world. Believe in it wholeheartedly, even though the road might not always be smooth, and you might need to make some tweaks along the way.

I recall a few months ago when my website was exceptionally playful and all about embracing the power of play. I soon realised that my message was too playful, and it was driving people away, but that's the beauty of this process. We need to play around with our ideas and work on them. I, too, had to take a step back and reflect on my original website. I had to acknowledge that it was perhaps too much for many. It might not have been as inclusive as I wanted it to be, and it wasn't fully authentic because my own brand of play is more subtle and uniquely me.

Play around with things, think big, but think big in your own way. This journey is yours - it's your life, your business, and your coaching practice. Aim for the stars, the rooftops, or wherever your dreams reside, but remember, it's essential to enjoy the process, to have fun along the way. Happiness is for today, for right now, not to be postponed until you reach the summit, earn a degree, land a promotion, or retire.

It is about savouring every step of your journey. Find joy in each day, embrace the power of playfulness, and be the person who isn't afraid to ride the electric bike through the city. Be the one who does things a bit differently and follows their heart. The foundation of coaching provides guidelines, ethics, and tools, but the magic happens when you intertwine it with your uniqueness.

So, if your coaching style could be anything, what would it be? If it were a superhero, who would it resemble? If it were an animal, what characteristics would it embody? The possibilities are endless, and that's what this journey is all about — unleashing your unique style, living your values, and making a difference in your way. Enjoy every moment of it, and remember, play is the key to unlocking your true potential and creating a ripple effect of happiness and success in your life and the lives of others.

ABOUT TAMZIN HALL

Tamzin Hall is a Performance Psychology Coach who helps leaders understand themselves and their team, navigate neurodiversity in the workplace and create a profitable workplace all while remaining professional and having fun.

Before starting a coaching business, Tamzin spent a decade as a leader and a performance manager in the banking and utility sectors.

After a successful career helping others to understand themselves better and achieve successful careers, Tamzin now helps business owners and leaders create teams that are high-performing, happy and successful.

Tamzin offers her expertise to assist leaders and business owners in fostering high-performing teams and gaining insights into their employees. She also conducts DISC workshops and training sessions aimed at enhancing communication, fostering understanding, and mitigating conflicts.

Tamzin enjoys watching her son play golf, walking her two dogs with friends and learning anything new!

You can reach Tamzin at:

Email: tamzin@tamzinhallcoaching.co.uk
Website: www.tamzinhallcoaching

instagram.com/tamzin_hall_coaching
linkedin.com/in/tamzin-hall

Printed in Great Britain
by Amazon

38966413R00126